In My Lifetime: An Odyssey of Supernatural Happenings

"*In My Lifetime* is stimulating, challenging, down-to-earth, biblically sound, and most of all Christ-honoring. If you are looking for sensationalism, you won't find it here. But if you are looking for the reality of the power and compassion of our Heavenly Father, you will find it in abundance. This book has my highest recommendation.
Jay Alford
Executive Presbyter, Assemblies of God
Senior Pastor
HIGHWAY TABERNACLE
Youngstown, Ohio

"...readable, heartwarming and a faith builder. I highly recommend it."
Philip Bongiorno
Superintendent
PENNSYLVANIA - DELAWARE DISTRICT
Assemblies of God

"Excellent reading!......a fascinating story of our miracle working God at work in the day to day challenges of life"
Rev. Carlton Spencer
Past President
Elim Fellowship & Elim Bible Institute
Lima, New York

"A Christian writer faces at least two formidable problems when writing a book like "In My Lifetime." First, the author must be careful that his readers are not more impressed by the writer than they are by the Lord.

"Second, there is a danger that the author will give the impression that he is superspiritual, that he has some special relationship with God that separates him from the more ordinary. Guy BonGiovanni has avoided both these pitfalls. One comes away from his book loving and trusting the Lord Jesus more and believing that crisis in his own life can be met by God."
Dr. Harold Helms
Vice Pres., Internat. Church of the Foursquare Gospel
Senior Pastor
ANGELUS TEMPLE
Los Angeles, California

In My Lifetime: An Odyssey of Supernatural Happenings

"It reminds one of the Book of Acts - its events and miracles....shows that Jesus is alive and still moves among His people today."
Daniel Ippolito
Gen. Supt., Italian Pentecostal Churches of Canada
Senior Pastor
HOWARD PARK PENTECOSTAL CHURCH
Toronto, Canada

"It is not often that you come across a book that shares intimate testimonies of the Lord's power and grace, and at the same time builds up your personal faith in God. This book will minister to your spirit and give you hope for the days ahead."
Rev. Paul Johansson
President, Elim Bible Institute
Lima, New York

"Very inspiring...desire to place this book in the hands of every member of our church, so that they would be able to understand and appreciate our rich heritage"
Rev. Larry Haynes
Senior Pastor
FIRST ASSEMBLY OF GOD
Farrell, Pennystvania

"This book will be a blessing...magnifies the sovereignty of God which is often overlooked."
Rev. Joseph M. Beretta
Superintendent
NEW JERSEY DISTRICT
Assemblies of God

"A masterpiece of wisdom revealed in real life experiences. Not theory! But practical events directed by the Holy Spirit showing God is alive in the street as well as in the sanctuary."
Sanford (Sandy) Kulkin
President
THE INSTITUTE FOR MOTIVATIONAL LIVING, INC.
New Castle, Pennsylvania

In My Lifetime

An Odyssey of Supernatural Happenings

2015 Second Edition

Guy BonGiovanni

Life Enrichment Ministries, Inc.
EMAIL: GuyBon1830@gmail.com

In My Lifetime: An Odyssey of Supernatural Happenings

In My Lifetime
God Events

Copyright © 1995 by Life Enrichment Ministries, Inc.,

All rights reserved. No part of this book may be reproduced, stored in a retrieval system, or transmitted in any form or by any means —electronic, mechanical, photocopy, recording, or otherwise— without prior written permission of the copyright owner, except brief quotations used in connection with reviews in magazines or newspapers. Requests for permission or information should be addressed in writing to Life Enrichment Ministries, Inc., P.O. Box 543, Hermitage, PA. 16159-6730.

Library of Congress Catalog Number: 95-94084

House of BonGiovanni
"Publishers of Good News"
ISBN 978-0-912981-28-4
2015 Second Edition

Cover Design: RGS Design, Sharon, PA.
Printed in the United States of America

Dedicated

*To Family,
Immediate and Extended,*

for

*Love, Support,
Understanding,*

and

*Their Good Will
In My
Pursuit Of Excellence
and
The Vision of God;*

Especially

*To
Frank,
My Esteemed Elder Brother*

*and
Dr. Nicholas J. Tavani,
My Lifetime Mentor and Friend.*

> *"And God is able to make all grace abound toward you; that ye, always having all sufficiency in all things, may abound to every good work"*
>
> 2 Corinthians 9:8

Table of Contents

Forward....................................11
Dr. Thomas F. ("Tommy") Reid
Preface....................................13
Dr. Nicholas J. Tavani
Introduction..........................17

Chapter 1 **My Wife and Daughter Spared By A Miracle At Childbirth** 23

Chapter 2 **Past Sixteen.... Still Very Much Alive!**............31

Chapter 3 **A Woman Who Wouldn't Wake Up**.................37

Chapter 4 **Doctors Didn't Expect Her To See Again**..............................45

Chapter 5 **Her Baby Turned Blue**..........................49

Chapter 6	**The Woman Who Dialed Her Telephone Supernaturally**	53
Chapter 7	**God Reshaped Her Deformed Feet**	57
Chapter 8	**Murder Was Lifted Out Of His Heart**	63
Chapter 9	**A Lost Daughter is Found**	69
Chapter 10	**Detoured Around a Terrorist's Bomb**	73
Chapter 11	**Doctors Said If The Child Lived Past Three, It Would Be a Miracle**	77
Chapter 12	**The Xray Told A Different Story**	81
Chapter 13	**In A Dream She Saw the Street and House Number**	85
Chapter 14	**Lions Walked into the Dining Room And The Mafia Hit Men Were Stopped**	89
Chapter 15	**When God Scuttled a Church Business Meeting**	95

Chapter 16 **The Mystery of Giving Money..
You Don't Have,
From Sources You
Don't Know About** *101*

Chapter 17 **How To Build a Home With No
Money for a Down Payment;
Yet, Have Enough Left Over to
Buy a Printing Plant**................. *111*

Chapter 18 **The Key To Purchasing
A Printing Company
On A Pastor's Salary**................ *125*

Chapter 19 **How to Sell a Business in a
Distressed Economy** *133*

Chapter 20 **An Unseen Energy Source
For Leadership**........................ *139*

Chapter 21 **What To Do
When The Lights Go Out**........... *151*

Epilogue:

I **Exclusive To The Thinking
Person**................................. *163*

II **A Bit About Myself** *175*

" Ye have not chosen me,
but I have chosen you,
and ordained you,
that ye should go
and bring forth fruit,
and that your fruit should remain:
that whatsoever ye shall ask
of the Father in my name,
he may give it you."
John 15:16

Forward

Often we "hear" what a preacher says, seldom do we know who a preacher "is." "In My Lifetime" is a look, not only at what a man has said, but a look into the life of the man, himself.

We all know the name of Guy BonGiovanni, a great pastor and preacher, denominational leader, writer, and Christian business man. However, for the first time we now learn what has developed the Christian character and worldview of the man behind the name. It is in this manuscript that we truly know the meaning when Paul, the apostle, calls us "Living Epistles."

"In My Lifetime" is a magnificant look at the triumphs of a man of faith. On these pages are described the miracles of faith Guy BonGiovanni has seen accomplished through the power of the Holy Spirit working in his life. On these same pages also are described the pain, the frustrations of strained relationships between brethren, and the knowledge of God's love and care in the midst of distressing and perplexing situations.

Here we see the wonder of honesty, the beauty of integrity, and the productivity of pain. Seldom does a man of God become so transparent. Because transparency demands honesty and integrity, however, this manuscript is a demonstration of two great Christian characteristics: honesty and integrity.

I commend to the Christian community the life of my brother, Guy BonGiovanni, and his magnificent honest portrait of the tragedies and triumphs of a great Christian leader, "In My Lifetime."

Dr. Thomas F. ("Tommy") Reid
Senior Pastor, The Tabernacle
Founder/President, Buffalo School of the Bible
Orchard Park, New York

Preface

For over forty years I have observed this man of incredible talents. His passion was to use them whenever and wherever God placed him, and I expect this will continue until God's period signals closure. It's expected the gifts God gives to us should be used to their maximum for His glory and the edification of the Church and society.

This book had to be written. Over half a century of service in the Church and University, I have observed a sense of anomie in people. Even persons of great talent, often because they are underused and less understood, find themselves in Bunyan's "slough of despond." Through supernatural happenings, as the author illustrates, our God encourages people to keep moving forward in life. This is what this odyssey is all about. In the course of living, come supernatural happenings to lift us up.

In My Lifetime: An Odyssey of Supernatural Happenings

As you read this book, you will wonder why you have not recognized how often God has worked on your behalf. Most of the supernatural happenings in our lives go unnoticed by most of us. We, consequently, fret because of our problems, instead of praise God because of our victories! As we recognize how often supernatural happenings have occurred imperceptibly in our lives, it will become obvious we cannot exaggerate God's Grace toward us.

Here are vignettes of exciting supernatural happenings. They are brief, understandable, engrossing situations with which you can identify. With a touch of levity, I can even say, the book is like the popular television commercial about a certain kind of potato chip which asserts, "I bet you can't eat one!" The combined taste of excitement and reality from one story will compel you to read another, then another and yet another - until, surprisingly, you have finished the whole book! This self-effacing, poignant account of God's interventions in a journey of faith will do it.

It happened to me! When I received the manuscript with a request to write this preface, I immediately wrote a letter saying I needed additional lead time. I was entering the hospital for by-pass surgery. I had a number of seminary papers to read, and a new semester was beginning at the University. Then I made a mistake! I thought I would read the introduction only and one chapter. But to my surprise, before I posted my letter, I was driven to read the whole book! It was compelling. I thought I should warn you!

Thank you, Guy, for taking me on this odyssey. It was a thriller and a lifter of my spirit.

N. J. Tavani, B.D., Ph.D.
Fort Washington, Maryland
January 11, 1995

*"And I, brethren,
when I came to you,
came not with excellency of speech
or of wisdom,
declaring unto you the testimony of God.
For I determined
not to know any thing among you,
save Jesus Christ, and him crucified....
And my speech and my preaching
was not with enticing words of man's wisdom,
but in demonstration of the Spirit and of power:
That you faith should not stand
in the wisdom of men,
but in the power of God."*
1 Corinthians 2:1-5

Introduction

For quite some time I've thought it might be inspirational to put in writing some of the unusual things that have happened over my lifetime because of faith. Without doubt, other people have had even greater experiences than I. But these are experiences, uniquely my own and which I can verify personally.

Things That "Must Not Be Left Unsaid"

I understand well that the motivation for a document with personal references easily can be misconstrued. As a matter of fact, that possibility repulsed me; and for years effectively inhibited this publication. In spite of that risk, however, I have come now to identify with Robert Schuller, who in his biography was quoted to say, "There are some things that have happened in my life I can take no credit for, but must not be left unsaid."

It was at least a year ago while resting in my bedroom in the home of Pastor Anthony Spero of Glen Burnie, MD., with whom I was having meetings, that I finally sensed a release to publish what you are about to read. I concluded the testimonies in this book "must not be left unsaid."

Although the book is not intended as autobiography, a considerable amount of autobiographical material is unavoidable. One of the final chapters, in fact, deliberately includes information about my personal background. I've always found it helpful and interesting to know something about the author of a book and I thought there might be others who share this interest. Hopefully, this bit of history about myself will make the book more enjoyable and meaningful to the reader.

The Frequency of Miracles

Like the works of God recorded in the Acts of the Apostles, the reader must be aware these supernatural happenings occurred over a long period of time. That's a fact we usually overlook when reading the New Testament. As a result, we tend to guilt-trip when supernatural things aren't happening every day in our walk with the Lord.

While there are special seasons that are punctuated by numerous miracles, we must understand that the normal course of life, by comparison, is only occasionally interspersed with the visibly supernatural. This doesn't in any way minimize the certainty of our Heavenly Father's presence and care. It only underscores that His daily help to us, more often than not, is channeled imperceptibly through more natural and less sensational avenues.

What should be apparent to the reader is that neither saint nor sinner leads a "charmed life." Job's "comforter" might have been overly cynical, but he faces the reality that "Man was born for trouble" (Job 5:7). Equally apparent is that when trouble comes, our Lord's care is available.

Supernatural intervention is possible. It happens! That doesn't mean everybody gets a miracle every time. But it does underscore, everybody is tenderly cared for by the One "who is touched with the feelings of our infirmities" (Heb. 4:15).

Wisdom, Power And Miracles
Nevertheless, if our faith is not to be shattered, perhaps one of the most important lessons we must learn is that God, Who is indeed powerful enough to do anything He wants to do, actually, does not always choose to work by that almighty power. He does always work, however, by His wisdom.

We have witnessed the supernatural works of God healing and helping people. But we also know of others who apparently were not healed or helped. Good people suffer and "bad" people seem to prosper. Some of our prayers are answered; others seem to fall upon deaf ears. It's not strange that this should either confuse or puzzle us. Clearly God *can* do it all! But, for reasons hidden within His wisdom, He doesn't do it. There is no supernatural intervention.

Lingering Questions
Unless one has disconnected his brain, something God never expects believers to do, questions will linger. But, ultimately, whether or not we understand everything that's going on is not important. Keeping one's faith steady is what's important. We might not understand it, but we can stand under it! The chapter on "What To Do When The Lights Go Out," is included in the book to help keep equilibrium during trouble. We must not forget, the same pressure that crushes the rock, creates the diamond. In the end, whether one shatters or shines, depends upon how well he takes the pressure.

The secret for standing under pressures we don't understand is a strong confidence in the *wisdom* of God. We can't reasonably doubt His love. His Word frequently assures us of it. And, again and again He has demonstrated it as the vignettes in this book illustrate. So, we can't doubt He will do what's best for us. Our basis for confidence in His wisdom, therefore, is solid, even if the specific miracle one needs doesn't happen.

Some of life's experiences always will be shrouded in mystery. Others inevitably will lead the thinking person to the conclusion that we are not alone. For what we can neither prove nor understand, we make no excuse. Gods, we are not! We are mere mortals and limited. For what is both understandable and historical, we make no apology. We simply bow our hearts in humility and give praise to our God and to His Christ, blest now and forevermore.

Through these accounts of the supernatural works of God, it is hoped the reader will grasp as the overriding message that our Lord is alive, that He cares deeply for you, and that He does good for those who sincerely seek, recognize and welcome Him.

With Appreciation
This book is offered with profound gratitude to the many people whose love and labors contributed so much to its completion. It is published with a deep sense of humility for the privilege of sharing in the miracles it records. In my heart there is an abiding prayer that the Christ, Who called me into His service so many years ago, shall be portrayed well to those who, with sincere heart

and mind, dare to explore and experience Him as He is, in fact: discoverable, accessible, and gracious —"the same yesterday, today and forever"— and in every sense, a *living* Friend.

In My Lifetime: An Odyssey of Supernatural Happenings

CHAPTER *1*

My Wife And Daughter Spared By A Miracle During Childbirth

After several months criss-crossing the Northeast in evangelistic meetings, Esther and I rented a small furnished three-room apartment in the Bronx, N.Y. The next big event in our lives was the arrival of our firstborn. Esther would be near her family, and I could shuttle back and forth to meetings without too much stress on either of us.

How we got the apartment and the terms was somewhat of a miracle of itself. We quickly traced every advertisement we saw of an available apartment. But apartments were scarce, especially on our "budget," and for the brief period needed.

We even followed a lead across the Hudson in Fort Lee. An elderly lady in Esther's home church told us about it. My brother Frank, who was working with the Rev. Ben Crandall in Brooklyn at the time, went along with us. It seemed we covered every street in the city, but couldn't find the place.

Finally, we inquired at a service station. No, the attendant didn't know where "Menna" street might be. In fact, he never heard of "Menna" street! There is a Main Street, he assured us, but no "Menna " street.

That's when the light went on! It finally dawned upon us the elderly Italian lady really was trying to say "Main" street! She just couldn't pronounce it right! We had a good laugh, found the apartment and returned to my in-laws. The apartment wasn't adequate. But the search did provide a bit of levity.

Somehow we learned an elderly couple would sub-let their apartment on Plymouth Avenue for a three-month trial period, possibly for six months if they found living in Florida helped Mr. Katrinick's asthma. The apartment was furnished. The rate and location, excellent. And the time-frame exactly what we needed for the baby's arrival. We were certain it was the Lord's provision.

On April 7th, 1956 the "Big Event" happened....with some surprises!

At 6:00 that morning, on April 7, 1956, Esther was awakened with labor pains. Her time had come. We hurriedly dressed and drove to Leff's Maternity Hospital on the Grand Concourse in the Bronx. Dr. Zietland, who had been Esther's family physician for years, was summoned.

In those days, husbands were not even permitted to be with their wives during labor, let alone in the delivery room. But I stayed with Esther until I was told to leave.

I can't say that I was overly nervous by what was happening. Esther and I were just two wide-eyed excited young people, anxiously expecting our new baby. That was all! We had not even a hint anything was wrong, or that something unpleasant might happen. It was just taking a long time, I thought.

Around 2:00 that afternoon, Dr. Zietland entered the waiting room. He still had on his surgical smock, and with his handkerchief was wiping his brow as he approached me. I rose to meet him, and quickly noticed a troubled look on his face.

"How did it go?" I asked.

The doctor passed his handkerchief across his forehead once again and rather soberly said, "It's all right now. Thank God, it's all right."

I was stunned. "What do you mean, 'It's all right now'?"

With great sensitivity, Dr. Zietland explained. The umbilical cord had been wrapped twice around the baby's neck. He had to use instruments to delicately turn the baby inside Esther's womb.

Dr. Zietland reassured me that both mother and baby were now doing well. Then he went on to express how fortunate we should feel, in spite of the difficult birth.

Normally, a mother's womb drops in preparation for a baby's passage through the birth canal. The length of the umbilical cord accommodates that procedure. For some unexplainable reason, however, Esther's womb had not dropped! If it had dropped, the good doctor explained, it would have killed both the baby and mother! I got a little weak as I realized I could have lost a child and become a widower in one moment. I was indeed fortunate, and grateful!

As I looked through the nursery window at the chubby little bundle of life safely cradled in the nurse's arms, my heart swelled with joy and gratitude. Standing at my side, my mother-in-law sounded like a percolator, sputtering and stammering her praise to God. If one had not been told, he would never suspect this child's recent brush with death. She held her head up although she wasn't even 24 hours old! And the exercise she was giving her lungs, as we watched, must have been "extra early boot camp" in preparation for her ministry in Gospel music that blesses so many today. It brought a healthy, rose-tinted glow to her 7lb.10 oz., nineteen inch vibrant body. We named her Linda, because she was indeed, beautiful.

A few days following Esther's return to our apartment, a letter arrived that was destined to underscore the Lord's care for us.

For a brief period following my training for the ministry, I traveled as an evangelist with Percy Benton of Norfolk, Virginia. Later he took an Associate Pastor position in the South and I continued in evangelistic ministry, and eventually married. In one of my letters I informed Percy that Esther and I were expecting a baby. The due date was projected at April 14, 1956. That was the only notice he had.

We hadn't heard from Percy for some time, so we hurriedly opened the letter. A sense of urgency seemed to drive Benton through the brief opening amenities of his letter. He wanted to know what was happening with Esther, and he explained the reason for his concern.

During the early morning hours of April 7th, fully one week ahead of Esther's due date, Mr. Benton was awakened from sleep. A deep burden for Esther's well-being in relation to the delivery of her baby nagged at his spirit. He was tired and wanted to sleep, he later told me, but the persistent nudging in his spirit wouldn't let him. He knew Esther was in trouble and needed prayer. Finally, he dragged himself out of bed and earnestly interceded for her until he was at peace about it, then returned to bed.

Now I understood why we had been so "fortunate." We had no idea of the danger lurking inside Esther's body. But our faithful Lord did! And in His mercy, He awakened from sleep a man, who was living at least 700 miles to the South, and led him to engage in the spiritual warfare that brought deliverance to Esther and our child.

Benton had never met my wife; never saw her picture; never talked with her by telephone. She was known to him only by my letter, informing him Esther would give birth on April 14, 1956, fully one week later than she did.

I can't explain it all. The Lord certainly was able to do it Himself! Why should He awaken Benton from sleep? Why was that praying necessary? Why get him involved at all?! There are no absolute answers.

What is important, is that our Lord cares for us. He knows even what we don't know about ourselves! For whatever reason it's necessary, He does call upon people to earnestly pray for our deliverance in our time of need. And because they pray, Somebody makes it happen. His name is Jesus!

"*Bless the LORD, O my soul:
and all that is within me,
bless his holy name.
Bless the LORD, O my soul,
and forget not all his benefits:
Who forgiveth all thine iniquities;
Who healeth all thy diseases;
Who redeemeth thy life from destruction;
Who crowneth thee with lovingkindness and
tender mercies;
Who satisfieth thy mouth with good things;
so that thy youth is renewed
like the eagle's.*
Psalm 103:1-5

CHAPTER **2**

Past Sixteen...
And Very Much Alive!!

Joan was born with a serious heart malady. Her mother told me both her family physician and specialists at the Cleveland Clinic were not too optimistic Joan would live with this condition beyond her sixteenth year. Apparently, that was the pattern science had observed in cases like hers.

Fortunately, Joan was born of a mother who not only knew the Lord, but also knew how to pray. In my frequent visits in her home she repeatedly said with a disarming simplicity as she faced her challenges, " We just trust in the Lord." And, indeed she did with respect to Joan, the youngest of her three daughters.

I vividly recall the occasion that seemed to be the turning point in Joan's well-being. She was regularly under doctor's care. But this time it was different. She was now about two years of age when she came down with what seemed to be a cold. During a precautionary check-up, her physician, Dr. Vermeire, reported he found evidence of infection around Joan's heart. In his professional judgment, it was serious enough to urge the family to take her to the Cleveland Clinic immediately. It happened on a weekend, so Joan's appointment in Cleveland was scheduled for Monday.

A family member presented her need for prayer during our Sunday evening service. I recall the experience vividly.

As the congregation stood, I asked Ralph Martino, an active layman in the Assembly, to offer the prayer in behalf of Joan. What followed was unusual; so unusual, in fact, that I don't recall it ever had happened before just like it did at that time, and it hasn't happened just like that since.

Our Lord said, "If any two of you shall agree on earth as touching any thing that they shall ask, it shall be done for them by my Father, who is in heaven" (Matt.18:19). The Amplified Bible is more lucid, and, in fact, quite descriptive of just what happened on that Sunday night. "Again I tell you, if two of you agree (harmonize together, together make a symphony) about — anything and everything — whatever they shall ask, it will come to pass and be done for them by My Father in heaven."

Our Lord's focus was on the need to be in "agreement" concerning what we ask of Him. That "agreement" is like a "symphony," a "harmonizing together" about the request we place before Him. The idea seems to be a profound sense of oneness, not particularily in the words that are spoken, nor in the posture taken, but a sense of oneness that knits soul-to-soul in an inexplicable harmony with the need we bring to God together. Although that level of kinship defies adequate description, if it ever happened, it happened that night as the Farrell Christian Assembly prayed for Joan Chiurazzi.

At the Cleveland Clinic, Joan's doctor examined her carefully. He was aware, of course, Joan's visit had been scheduled as an emergency. But all seemed to be in order. Baffled that she should be sent for emergency examination when she was apparently in good health for her condition, the Clinic doctor telephoned Dr. Vermeire.

"Why did you send Joan to me for examination?" he asked.

Dr. Vermeire explained. "When I examined her, Joan had a serious infection in the region of her heart. I concluded It was serious enough to require your attention."

"Well, I don't know what you found in your examination," replied the specialist as he closed the conversation, "but I can tell you there is absolutely nothing wrong with Joan at the present time."

Part of the entry in my personal Journal for April 17, 1962 reads, "Geri Chiurazzi phoned to inform that Joan is declared A-OK by physcian in Cleveland. Amazed at the Chiurazzies for bringing her prematurely for her check-up since he found no reason to do so. When informed Dr. Vermeire urged the quick appointment because of infection and failing symptoms in (Joan's) heart, he called Vermeire for information. Dr. Vermeire said he couldn't understand it, but when he checked, her symptoms were alarming. Obviously, Jesus healed her! Thank God."

That was about thirty years ago. During the intervening time, Joan has grown to be a fine young lady, active and happy. She graduated high school, took managerial training and managed for some time a Thrift Drug store in the Shenango Valley. Currently, she is in management with Wal Mart.

The little girl, who it was feared might be dead by the age of sixteen, is living testimony that prayer is powerful; that the Great

Physician does intervene supernaturally to help us. There is, indeed, tremendous power to achieve great things when people of Faith agree together in prayer.

*" I waited patiently
for the Lord:
and he inclined unto me,
and heard my cry.
He brought me up also
out of an horrible pit,
out of the miry clay,
and set my feet upon a rock,
and established my goings.
And he hath put a new song
in my mouth,
even praise unto our God;
many shall see it, and fear,
and shall trust in the LORD. "*
Psalm 40:1-3

CHAPTER 3

A Woman Who Wouldn't Wake Up

It was a time scheduled for celebration at the Christian Assembly of Ecorse, Michigan, where I was the guest speaker. But it was a time of unsuspected challenge to the faith of the John Apa family in Farrell, Pa.

The Apas were members of the Farrell Christian Assembly which I served as pastor. They had served the Lord for many years and were widely respected for their Christian commitment. John Jr. operated our small church printing press, served as the Superintendent of Records and Evaluation for our growing Sunday School, and later as a trustee of the church. Joanne was not as active as her brother, but occasionally contributed her artistic skills. Antoinette was a minister's wife and Brother John Apa, Sr., a tall, distinguished gentleman of few words, served as one of the three deacons of the church. His steady commitment brought him to the church at 8:00AM daily for prayer with Brothers Anthony Chiodo and Mike Cagno, our other deacons. Often, in the course of my pastoral calls, weaving in and out of the Shenango Valley streets, I would come upon him, casually walking across our Valley distributing miniature Gospels of John to everyone he met. He had a great heart for leading people to Christ.

Life plays no favorites, however. And the faith of this family would be tested severely in spite of their Christian commitment. Of itself, that would be nothing new to the Apas.

In earlier years, Mr. Apa had been severely tested. An unusual eye malady fell upon his wife. Because it paralyzed her optic nerve, it was impossible for her to keep visual focus. No medical treatment was available for the sickness. I understand Mr. Apa already had been told that Jesus came not only to save, but also to heal people of their physical infirmities. But at that point, he, as yet, had not committed his life to Christ. Now that the doctors claimed his wife could be healed by God alone, the moment of decision was suddenly upon him. He would test the reality of the Message he heard. Without fanfare, Mr. Apa trusted Christ and his wife was healed!

Now, years later and in advanced age, Mrs. Apa again lay within the grip of a mysterious illness. She was admitted to the Sharon General Hospital where I called on her on my way to the airport enroute to Michigan. Though obviously ill, Mrs. Apa was lucid and resting well. After prayer, she bade me good-bye with the quiet smile that usually graced her face. All was at peace and she would heal with time —so I thought, as I confidently left for the airport.

The Michigan congregation was justifiably excited about their relocation to Lincoln Park and dedication of their new sanctuary. A packed church listened intently to the Word of the Lord and enthusiastically celebrated the historic occasion. The Lord was present to heal and to bless as we continued nightly services through the week.

When I called home early in the week, Esther informed me of Mrs. Apa's condition. Shortly after I left her on Saturday, she lapsed into something like a coma. It was puzzling and disconcerting.

Reports reaching me through the week were not encouraging, and a deep spirit of prayer came upon me. I couldn't shake it day or night. I spent a lot of time before the Lord in her behalf. In fact, it seemed to me I was waging spiritual warfare for her very life. A holy anger against Satan and sickness rose up in my spirit. It built in intensity as each day passed, and reports of her condition did not improve. At times as I prayed, the depth of the anointing made me feel like I was ten feet tall, taking authority over the situation in the name of the Lord Jesus Christ.

Whether or not it was in vision, I don't know. But at one point, a holy boldness rose up within me and birthed with it was a strong conviction that, as I entered Mrs. Apa's hospital room upon my return, the mysterious illness would be defeated by the grace and power of God, and lift my sister from her coma! It was as though I had been clothed with special, but unexplainable, authority from the very Throne of God.

A few days later, I flew home and drove from the airport directly to the hospital. As I approached Mrs. Apa's room, that strong authority I sensed a few days past, again came over me with unmistakable impact. As I entered the room, it was as though I was encapsulated within "Somebody bigger —much, *much* bigger than I." I knew God was there to bring healing!

Just as I reached her bedside, as though on cue, Mrs. Apa's eyes opened. She came out of the coma! My impression was that "the anointing (broke) the yoke" of sickness. In the purposes of God for Mrs.

Apa, that sickness could no more continue in her body than the image of Dagon, the false god, could stand in the presence of the Ark of the Lord. Something mysterious and miraculous apparently happened in the invisible realm that somehow connected the anointing I sensed with the moment of her deliverance.

It was a delight to see her smile, hear her voice and chat for a moment as though we were merely picking up our conversation where we left off several days past, as if nothing had intervened. The next day she was discharged.

I recounted to Esther the wrestlings of my spirit during the past week, and the timing of Mrs. Apa coming out of her "sleep" as I entered her room. I said to her it was as though, when I left her, Mrs. Apa just decided to close her eyes for a rest and wait until I returned before she would open them again! Of course, that really wasn't the case. It just *seemed* so.

Quite frankly, I can't understand it all. There are depths of reality here we know very little about. I just know this kind of thing happens. And the extent to which miraculous happenings are connected to a minister's presence leads people in some cultures to assign values to their minister's presence that appear quite extreme to many in our culture.

Some years ago, when I was walking through an open market in Kumasi, Ghana, Africa with my host pastor, for example, a member of his great church asked me to say a prayer for God's blessing over her business. Of course, I was happy to oblige. But I was not prepared for the significance this woman would attach to my prayer. I noticed as I was about to pray, the woman suddenly became quite verbal, making gestures that clearly indicated something was wrong. I didn't understand her language. But I knew I had missed something very important to her.

My host smiled as he explained the woman wanted me to step *inside* her booth and say the blessing. He further explained the people believe the blessing of God accompanies the man of God; that the ground he steps upon is blessed of God like the Book of Joshua says. So, she wanted me *inside*, rather than outside. She wanted God's blessing in her business and believed she would have it if the man of God stepped inside.

One must be extremely careful about reading into this tradition anything super special. But, I have enough "Episcopalian" in me to recognize, without question, that the ministry is *different!* The New Testament does set ministers apart from other believers, not with respect to merit, but with regard to role. The ground is level for all at

Calvary. But the Call to ministry is distinctive. Shepherds differ from the sheep. Whatever else might be read into this uniqueness, it seems to be a basic fact of Christianity that God's special blessing rests upon those whom He selects for ministry. We mustn't either demean it or delight in it. It's what is, that's all!

Laban was quite vocal in recognizing this distinction as he tried to persuade Jacob to continue as a member of his household: "I have learned by experience that the Lord hath blessed me *for thy sake*" (Gen.30:27). Even though they had some squabbles, the prosperity Laban came into with Jacob at his side, could not be ignored easily. There was something special about him that Laban didn't want to lose.

A suggestion of this same uniqueness was apparent when the Lord said to Joshua, "Every place that the sole of your foot shall tread upon, that have I given unto you, as I said unto Moses" (Joshua 1:3). And the disciples of Jesus, set apart for His service, were pointedly instructed by our Lord to "bless" or "withhold the blessing" in homes they visited, according to how they were received. An indisputable uniqueness rested, not only upon the mission, but also upon the men, when our Lord *set them apart* to His service. That's what it means to be "ordained" to the ministry (John 15:16).

There is no way we can know, empirically, whether any or none of this, had any bearing on the sudden awakening of Mrs. Apa when I entered her hospital room. There is therefore no reason, on the one hand for self-adulation, or on the other, for self-deprecation. What is certain is what happened. That much is unequivocal. And we celebrate that reality for the glory of God.

CHAPTER **4**

Doctors Didn't Expect Her To See Again

She was a little lady. Even I stood taller, and I'm not a "six-footer." Yet, there was a greatness in her that spoke more loudly than physical stature could.

Often as I greeted worshippers leaving our church sanctuary, she stood to the side, waiting for her daughter and son-in-law. In my memory, I can yet see her standing there, glowing...just glowing! An almost mystical radiance surrounded her as she calmly cast the warmth of her smile....now to this one, and then to that one... as each passed by. She didn't move, rarely said a word. She only smiled, and glowed!

Although Mrs. Madasz was not a member of our Assembly, because of her rather frequent visits, she was deeply loved by our congregation. So, it was not surprising that this little Hungarian woman became the subject of intense prayer during our services just as soon as we learned she must undergo surgery for cataracts, a much more serious surgical procedure in the sixties than it is today.

I was with her before surgery. With her loved ones at her bedside, we asked the Great Physician to take care of her as we entrusted her to the skills of her chosen surgeon. And we had confidence that He would.

Not always does the Lord heal apart from the medical profession. The Apostle Paul was forthright in telling the Romans that civil authorities are *ministers of the Lord* (Romans 13:4). Often medical personnel are as much ministers of the Lord for the healing of our bodies, as civil servants are for the peace of society. And it was with this confidence Mrs. Madasz underwent surgery. So, we felt quite confident in commending her to the Lord even though the prognosis was not encouraging.

The morning after Grandma Madasz's surgery, the nurse serving her was in for a big surprise! I recall from my pastoral days of "making rounds" at the Sharon General Hospital, that while most nurses wore white uniforms, for some reason, a few dressed in pink outfits. That was the case with Mrs. Madasz's nurse that morning.

She gently unwrapped the dressing from her patient's eye and turning to dispose of it heard something she never expected. If her patient's vision would return at all, she knew, it would be limited at best. In fact, there really was no great hope she would see from that eye again. But what the nurse was hearing indicated something radically different was happening.

Grandma Madasz had quietly remarked, "That's a pretty pink dress you are wearing."

In startled unbelief, the nurse turned to see if that voice, indeed, had come from her patient. Assured that it had, she dashed down the corridor, calling for the doctor. It reminded me of the woman in the Bible, who having had a dramatic encounter with Jesus, ran into the village shouting, "Come, see!"

Excitement raced among the other patients and staff. And understandably! What happened was not supposed to happen. In fact, just the opposite was the more likely prospect. Surgery had been a "best efforts" attempt at salvaging something that was more than not lost to this lovely lady with a glowing face.

The medical profession had predicted Mrs. Madasz, at best, only would see images vaguely; at worst, she would be blind. The nurse's reaction was understandable. Something had happened here beyond medical science. By every indication her patient had been touched by the miraculous power of the Great Physician, and it was mind boggling.

The completeness and speed of her recovery were a marvel to Mrs. Madasz's physicians. Her son, John, who owned and operated a successful funeral home in nearby Brookfield, Ohio called the family together to witness this unusual, but welcome happening. What they had expected to be an adjustment to blindness, turned out to be a time of celebration for sight restored, because Jesus passed by!

CHAPTER 5

Her Baby Turned Blue

Norma was having a hard time believing what she just heard. She was a fine woman and a recent Christian. But this was a little too much! She thought God couldn't possibly be as personal as the church member described in her testimony.

There was no question about the service last Sunday night. It was really a powerful move of God. But *why* or *how* would the Lord reveal all this ahead of time to the woman who testified? Could it really be that God revealed to her all about the unusual sense of God's presence we had Sunday night?

The service had been extraordinary, all right. But the dream Mrs. Staul claimed, must have been sheer coincidence. Things like this...*prophetic* dreams...were a thing of the past. God doesn't communicate with people so sensationally anymore. Anyway, if Norma were to believe it, the Lord would have to prove it to her personally. And He did!

Wash day came around with typical regularity. But this one was destined to be different. Norma placed her three-month old Jamie on the bed upstairs, and gently tucked the blanket about her as most mothers would, before going outside to hang the wash.

The neighborhood seemed to be pervaded with a peaceful stillness. The freshness of the early morning air brought Norma a relaxing sense of well being.

Then it happened! The solitude of her work was mysteriously broken by what she thought was a gentle calling out of her name.

"Norma," said the voice.

She pushed back the sheets on her clothes line, thinking her neighbor called. But no one was there. "I must be hearing things," she thought as she returned to her wash. But it happened again. Only her name was called more forcefully this time.

Now she was really perplexed. Norma thoroughly scoured the area to see who might be calling. But she found no one. Frustrated, almost to the point of anger; yet embarrassed at the playfulness of her imagination, Norma again threw herself feverishly into completing the wash.

What happened from that point was destined to change Norma's attitude about God's intimate concern for an individual, and the sensational nature of His guidance at times. The voice almost thundered this time, but with a frightening addendum.

"Norma! Your baby is choking!"

The basket in her hand dropped to the ground. First in shock, then in panic, Norma raced into the house and up the stairs. A momentary pause on the landing to hear the baby breathing brought only a spine chilling silence. She bolted up the remaining stairs and into the bedroom

Her eyes bulged in panic at what she saw. Her baby already had turned blue from lack of oxygen. It was the longest moment of her life as Norma frantically wrestled with the blanket, now twisted tightly around Jamie's neck and head. She finally jerked the last knot free and oxygen poured into the baby's lungs. The sound of rushing air was like music to the desperate mother. She got there in time, not only to save her baby's life, but to prevent the possibility of brain damage as well.

It was a harrowing experience. But the baby's big breath of air did more than restore Jamie's life. It also became the breath of life for the faith of a woman who questioned how intimately...and dramatically, at times...God does care for His people.

CHAPTER 6

The Woman Who Dialed Supernaturally

It was on a Wednesday afternoon. I was deeply into my preparation for an evening Bible Study. The ring of the telephone was about to lead me into the strangest telephone conversation I had ever experienced.

A lady's subdued voice whispered without introduction, "Will you pray for me?"

The request startled me and momentarily left me speechless. When I recovered I asked a few questions of my own. What is the problem? Don't you have a church home? Have you called your pastor?

In the next few moments I learned the lady was a Christian. She, indeed, was a church member and had a faithful pastor. Her problem was that she feared what seemed to be a recurrence of a serious heart problem.

Just recently she had been discharged from Sharon General following several days of treatment there. But now, she was getting the same severe chest pains she had before going to the hospital. She needed help!

When I asked her why she hadn't called her own pastor, her answer moved me deeply. "You see," she said, " I'm blind. I don't know my pastor's number and I can't see to find it in the directory." Now I was really puzzled.

"Well, how did you come to dial my number?" I asked.

She seemed to speak even a bit more softly now, as if in reverent recognition that she had been part of something that was tremendously awesome in its supernatural implications. I was in no way prepared for her comment. "I just lifted the receiver with a prayer in my heart that the good Lord would direct my fingers to dial the number of a man who could pray a prayer of deliverance for me."

I was stunned! You can only imagine the rush of mixed emotions, as amazement intertwined with deep confidence. I realized that, in that very moment, the soft-spoken woman and I were players in the unfolding of one of God's miracles.

When I recovered from the initial shock, we prayed and the lady got to shouting! I called back through the telephone, "Are you all right? Are you all right?"

"Yes, thank God!" she shouted. "And the pain is all gone!"

It was almost too much to believe, except I was there and I couldn't deny it. What a tribute to the loving concern of our Heavenly Father! And what a demonstration of the fact that "Jesus Christ (is) the same yesterday, and today, and forever" (Hebrews 13:8). We must never forget it. The Lord knows not only *what* we are facing; He also knows *how* to get us help.

Some time later I learned the woman was a Mrs. Delany, the widow of a local pastor and a very devout Christian.

One more little blessing completes this unusual demonstration of the Living Christ. I told this remarkable story while addressing a men's prayer breakfast in the Sharpsville Presbyterian church, served at the time by my dear friend, Dr. Sloan.

As I finished my message, Rev. Gillespi of Sharpsville, Pa. stood and respectfully said, "Brethren, please indulge me for a moment. I want to confirm what Brother BonGiovanni just said about Mrs. Delany.

I've heard her testify many times during services of how the Lord brought healing to her. God did a wonderful work of healing in her body like Brother BonGiovanni said."

Why the Lord does what He does, in the way that He does...is often puzzling to us. Fortunately, we are not called to understand and explain everything. Some things are best just accepted!

In meeting the challenges in life, the Bible assures us, "we have not an high priest which cannot be touched with the feeling of our infirmities." We are, therefore, encouraged to "come boldly unto the throne of grace, that we may obtain mercy, and find grace, to help in time of need" (Hebrews 4:15,16).

CHAPTER 7

God Reshaped Her Deformed Feet

They were a handsome couple. Jim had the impeccable "ivy league" look with winning personality to match. Marie was a fun-loving, beautiful woman. Both were model material. Both were full of life and lived it fully.

As a consultant with Sears Corporation, Jim was assigned, generally, to a troubleshooting role at their new installations, with the result that he and Marie relocated quite frequently. Eventually, they were assigned to the new Shenango Valley Sears store.

For this young couple climbing to the top of the corporate ladder, this latest assignment was especially a pleasure. It brought them back home to the Youngstown,

Ohio area where they would be closer than usual to family and friends.

As a boy, Jim had been active in his home church in Youngstown. Marie, on the other hand, although related to a church by heritage, had never personally committed her life to Christ.

My first call on the Capos, who recently had arrived in Sharon, was at the request of a relative. Although the visit was cordial, Jim and Marie were not particularly fond of having the preacher call on them. At the time their personal relationship was quite strained. As Jim sometimes comments in telling his story, there were occasions when they had to cut their bickering and "duck" because the preacher was at the door!

As the months wore on, I kept returning to the home of these hospitable, but reluctant friends. Eventually Jim renewed his commitment to Christ. Shortly afterward, Marie invited Jesus to be both Savior and Lord of her life. They developed beautifully in the Lord. But the day came when they were transferred to Steubenville, Ohio, a steel city about an hour distant from us.

During one of their occasional return visits with us, the Lord did something unusual and miraculous for them. It was on an

Easter Sunday. People, newly committed to Christ, were being baptized in water and Marie, who had never been baptized as a believer, also followed her Lord in baptism.

Added to the joy of the occasion, was the blessing of meeting the Capo's firstborn. Lisa was a beautiful baby, perfect in every detail, except one. Her parents told me she had been born with club feet and requested prayer for her healing.

Every available means for Lisa's help was being pursued. But, Jim and Marie looked to the Lord for her healing. They believed the same Lord Who turned their lives around was also the Great Physician to Whom nothing is impossible. He could heal Lisa's legs, too.

That Easter Sunday, after baptizing Marie in water, we lifted little Lisa Marie to the Lord Jesus Christ in Christian dedication. We asked Him, not only to cover her life with His blessing, but also to touch her little feet with the mighty power of His resurrection.

The Word of the Lord was clear to us. He had said through His servant Paul, "If the Spirit of him that raised up Jesus from the dead dwell in you, he ....shall also quicken your mortal bodies by his Spirit that dwelleth in you" (Romans 8:11). We wanted Him to show again the quickening power of His resurrection which we celebrated on that day.

And He did it ! Lisa's legs straightened-out in a remarkable way. Even her physician was amazed at her development. Not a trace of the impediment remained. Clearly, the Lord performed a miracle!

Lisa developed into a lovely young woman. Her legs haven't even a hint of deformity. In fact, she also is "model material," virtually a clone of her mother. Today she is happily married to Keith Lockhardt, a professional baseball player formerly with the Oakland A's Minor League team and at this writing playing in Caracas, Venezuela. Both are deeply involved in Christian service.

Understandably, the impact of Lisa's healing left a continuing positive influence upon the Capo family. Years later, following their preparation for ministry at Rhema Bible Institute in Tulsa, Oklahoma, Esther and I spent an overnight with the Capos. They were living in Washington, D.C. at the time. (Jim later went on to serve as a pastor in St. Petersburg, Florida.)

While standing in the foyer of their Washington, D.C. home, looking through an old Bible that had been part of the furnishings in the U.S. Senate, I was reminded of Lisa's healing. Lisa's younger brother joined me.

He stood there quietly, examining me from head to toe as closely as I was examining the antique Bible. He couldn't have been more than five at the time. He said nothing. Just stood there looking!

Suddenly, he broke silence. " Are you the man who prays?" he bluntly asked. That's all he said, looking up at me as though waiting for some great pronouncement.

Frankly, I didn't know how to react to his question. It was really cute, and my first impulse was to laugh. But as I looked down into the sincerity in his innocent eyes, I knew immediately that wouldn't be appropriate. His parents obviously had told him the story of Lisa's healing in anticipation of our visit. Perhaps this was his way of telling me he knew about it.

We spoke of it again for a few minutes. It was a heartwarming moment. Apparently he was satisfied. He heard about the miracle. He saw it for himself. He talked with the man who prayed. That was enough! And Jimmy walked off.

*For God so loved the world,
that he gave his only begotten Son,
that whosoever believeth in him
should not perish,
but have everlasting life.
For God sent not his Son
into the world
to condemn the world;
but that the world
through him
might be saved."*
John 3:16,17

CHAPTER **8**

Murder Was Lifted Out Of His Heart

The telephone call was a pleasant surprise. It originated from St. Louis, Mo. but the voice was distinctively Ghanaian. Six weeks earlier I said my goodbyes to Sarpong, my eloquent interpreter during my mission to Ghana. We hoped to hear from him again, but had no idea it would be this soon!

We were thrilled to learn someone covered his travel and lodging expenses to the Full Gospel Businessmen's Convention in St. Louis; so, we hurriedly packed-up our two young daughters, traveled to St. Louis and enjoyed the convention with Sarpong.

It was while sitting in the hotel lobby during a break between services that Sarpong leaned forward in his chair and said, "Brother, I must tell you what happened in Tema. If I don't tell you, you will have no way of knowing." What followed explained my inner struggle as we traveled that night from Accra, the capital city to Tema, a city several miles to the South.

Our auto bumped along the road as we sped toward the meeting site. The roads weren't the best, but I was more uncomfortable in my spirit.

It seemed the Lord was leading me to speak to the people about the woman taken in adultery. I wasn't too happy with the idea. I knew the stereotype abroad of the "Ugly American," who related to nationals in a condescending manner. The stereotype was repulsive to me. It might be suspected I was inferring Africans were more immoral than Americans if I preached that message. I wanted no part of that. I didn't want to give reason for my precious African friends to even suspect I might be part of that image. I struggled with it. But finally did what a servant of God must do. I bent my will to do God's will. And as Sarpong unfolded the drama that went on beneath the surface of that public gathering, I was grateful I had obeyed the Lord.

Sometime before that meeting a young African school teacher was transferred to the North Country. That assignment would separate him from his wife for several months. Economic constraints dictated it was the thing to do; so amid the usual tears of separation, he left for his new assignment, fully intending to return after several months.

But circumstances unexpectedly changed. A month or two later he was back in Tema, trying to locate his wife, who mysteriously no longer was living in their home. None of the neighbors seemed to know where she might be. In fact, they were visibly quite uncomfortable as the young husband inquired of them. No one would really talk with him about his wife.

Ultimately, a Christian gentleman saw his dilemma, and with as much delicacy as possible told the young man about his wife. Apparently, the woman desperately wanted children. But for some reason she could not conceive with her husband. Her plan was to live with another man while her husband was away. He wouldn't know about it, and on his return the problem would be solved. She would have "his" baby! But it was not to be.

The young man was furious. He purchased a cutlass and pledged to kill both his unfaithful wife and her lover. It seemed nothing could placate his rage. In a desperate attempt to avoid the carnage, the Christian gentleman pled with the enraged husband.

"Please do just one thing for me before you do this thing!" he said. "An American missionary will speak at our church tonight. Come and hear him first. It can't hurt you. And, after, if you still think what you want to do is right, then go do it."

Our car moved into the service site. The gathering was between two school buildings. There was no overhead covering, just the stars. A few lights had been strung here and there to prevent people from stepping on one another. This was their church.

I was told the people numbered around a thousand that evening. But one person whom I would never meet was of special importance. There was good liberty in worship and in preaching. As usual Sarpong stood at my side, always quick with the interpretation of my statements. He kept right with me as I told the congregation about the forgiveness Jesus brought to the woman taken in the very act of adultery, and explained our need to follow his example. Many people responded to the invitation to accept Christ as Savior. But something special happened to the young husband sitting there, burning with murderous rage in his heart.

With deep emotion Sarpong quietly shared with me how the young husband, himself, later described it. "While the American missionary was speaking," he said, "it seemed like a big hand reached down inside of me, and slowly lifted the anger up, up, and out of my body until it was all gone. I was free!" He no longer needed his cutlass. Jesus changed his life.

The anger was dissipated. The intent to kill left. Forgiveness flooded his heart where murder once raged. The powerful Word of God broke the chains of hate, preserved life and restored that marriage.

It was the kind of thing that underscores the wisdom of following the leadership of the Lord, in spite of how uncomfortable one might feel about it. At the same time, it brought a great sense of affirmation of my relationship to God, in that the Scripture declares, "as many as are led by the Spirit of God, they are the sons of God" (Romans 8:14). It took a trip from Accra, Ghana to St. Louis for Sarpong to point it out, but it was undeniable. What I had sensed in my heart, indeed, had been the leading of the Lord!

*"Come unto me,
all ye that labour
and are heavy laden,
and I will give you rest.
Take my yoke upon you,
and learn of me;
for I am meek
and lowly in heart:
and ye shall find rest
unto your souls.
For my yoke is easy,
and my burden is light."*
Matthew 11:28-30

CHAPTER *9*

A LOST DAUGHTER FOUND

During the years I was Director of Missions for the Christian Church of North America, a woman telephoned to see if we could help locate the daughter of her Lutheran friend. We were a logical place to begin her search because they thought the lost daughter had joined a missions team that came through our Valley a year before. She hadn't been heard from since.

Neither I nor others on our staff had knowledge of the missions team. But I assured the woman our staff would be coming together in a few moments for our daily time of prayer. We would join with her in prayer for the Lord's intervention.

While we were praying, suddenly my mind was flooded — that's the best way I can describe it — with the name of a man whom I had met at least three years earlier. He happened to be the director of a mission in a not-too-distant city. But, our paths had not crossed over the years and only few times since had thoughts of him crossed my mind. A strong impulse to telephone him about the lost girl accompanied the flooding of my mind with his memory.

The focus of my colleagues' mission was on oriental evangelism. In my earlier visit to his headquarters, in fact, I noticed a number of his staff were Orientals. I telephoned immediately upon closing our staff prayers.

The receptionist answering the telephone was obviously a young person. She was pleasant as she informed me the Director of the Mission was unavailable. At the moment he was in the Orient. I was disappointed, thinking I had made the call in vain.

I was about to close my conversation with the young woman when suddenly my mind was again flooded with a strong impulse to ask the young lady her name. Normally, I wouldn't have been so forward. But the sense of the Lord's anointing provided the necessary boldness. And I'm so glad I did! The young lady graciously told me her name —and the lost girl was found!

Esther and I can empathize, in a small measure, with parents whose children have vanished. For a fleeting moment, but what seemed like an eternity, we had lost our three year old granddaughter. The flashes of anxiety that slashed back and forth inside us during those long minutes could only be a microcosm of the profound pain suffered by parents with long-term lost children. Nonetheless, our pain was real.

We brought Stacey with us to a local furniture store. As we stepped out of the elevator, she suddenly broke free, dashed around a partition directly in front of the elevator and disappeared!

She had no idea of potential danger. Everyone was her friend. We raced around the partition to interrupt her playful maneuver. But she was gone! It was only three or four seconds. But she disappeared...like she vanished. It happened so fast!

Had she run through another door...fallen through an opening in the floor - perhaps through a furnace grating in the old building? Had someone, lurking behind the partition snatched her away? A million possibilities race through one's imagination at a time like that.

We quickly alerted security as we raced through the floor and through connecting departments. She was nowhere to be found.

Then a thought popped into my mind: crunch down to floor level -just about Stacey's height- and as far as I could see, without obstruction of furniture, look for the playful little girl hiding under a table. I had done it quickly before. But now I must look more carefully, deliberately.

And there she was. Her tiny body almost blended with the single post of a distant circular table. We were frantic. But she was having fun!

The relief we experienced at that moment is what every sensitive person would hope for parents whose children are missing. Whether it's a lost coin (Luke 15:9), a lost axe head (2 Kings 6:5), a lost sheep (Luke 15:4), or a lost child (Luke 15:24), the Good Shepherd knows where it is. Of Him, the psalmist testified, "thy rod and thy staff they comfort me" (Psalm 23:4). He can help you, too!

CHAPTER **10**

Detoured Around a Terrorist's Bomb

It hasn't been too long ago that Esther and I were reminded dramatically of our Lord's watchful care over us. We had just completed ministry at the ADI Convention (Assemblies of God) in Naples, Italy and were preparing for the next leg of our ministry tour in Northern Europe.

We were originally scheduled to fly out of Rome into Frankfurt, Germany for a convention. Friends, whom we met in Naples and who were scheduled for that same convention, however, invited us to travel by car with them. It was a nice thought. But, it was logistically impossible.

Without a luggage carrier, there was no way we could pack four adults with baggage, into a small European car for such a long trip. And none seemed available. We finally decided to accompany them as far as Pisa, then travel separately the longer distance to Frankfurt.

We said our goodbyes. But as we were entering the vehicle for the first leg of our journey, a young man came running around the corner of the house shouting, " I found a luggage carrier! I found a luggage carrier! "

Not until our arrival in Germany did we realize this last minute discovery actually saved our lives. News media were alive with reports of a terrorist explosion in the Frankfurt terminal. The bomb that killed several people and dismembered others in one of the worst carnages in memory, exploded in the baggage area at precisely the scheduled arrival time of our flight. But, thank God, we weren't there!

Who would have suspected the Creator of the universe might have orchestrated even the discovery of that luggage carrier so our lives could be spared? We certainly hadn't!

There had been no voice, audible or perceived; no uneasiness of spirit; no "prophetic" word; no dream –nothing unusual or dramatic, either to alert us of danger or assure us of special direction. Only a quiet, unnoticed steering of our path away from danger.

The God, Who wove His way in and out of centuries of major and mundane human events to protect His Messianic seed, also had spared our lives with a last-minute discovery of a luggage carrier! And we are grateful.

*"Is any sick among you?
let him call for the elders
of the church;
and let them pray over him,
anointing him with oil
in the name of the Lord:
And the prayer of faith
shall save the sick,
and the Lord
shall raise him up
....and pray one for another
that ye may be healed.
The effectual fervent prayer
of a righteous man
availeth much."*
James 5:14-16

CHAPTER 11

Doctors Said If The Child Lived Past Three It Would Be a Miracle

At this writing, John Andrew Hempstead must be twenty years of age. What's significant about this is that according to medical science he should have been dead seventeen years ago! And he would have been, had it not been for the supernatural intervention of the Lord.

John's parents, John, Sr. and Claudia, had done the drug scene for years, and actually were on drugs throughout Claudia's pregnancy. Concerned for the effect the drugs might have on Claudia's child, her physician suggested an abortion. Claudia refused. She already was the mother of two and they were healthy. So, she would risk it with her third child. It was a decision she would later question, but one she believed was correct from the beginning.

John Andrew was born with Soton Syndrome. Soton is similar to Downs Syndrome, but as Pat Leali, who interviewed the Hempsteads for a religious magazine put it, "with an added twist. With Soton, a child's head is abnormally large and continues to expand until it bursts, causing death."

The Hempsteads did everything humanly possible to help their young son. A neurologist in New York saw him for two years. His condition was hopeless. Normally, a child with Soton Syndrome is not expected to live beyond three years. If he does, he must be institutionalized.

During this time of acute struggle for the Hempsteads, their pastor, the Rev. Emanuel Greco of Brooklyn, N.Y., scheduled a spiritual emphasis weekend with me. The people gathered in large numbers and God's Spirit moved dramatically. Many people received the Baptism in the Holy Spirit that weekend.

Claudia and her husband, John, were deeply committed Christians at the time, although they had only recently accepted Christ as their Savior and Lord. Their lives were open to what God wanted of them; and they looked to Him for help with their special challenges. At the time, however, neither of them was aware that healing was available for their son through the Atonement of Jesus.

It was more of a family thing, that young John was with them in church that night, rather than an intentional seeking for his healing. Healing, as so much more in the Christian life, was new to them. Nevertheless, they responded when an invitation for healing was given.

For the ministry of healing that night, the congregation was asked to stand. Those needing healing were further instructed to raise their hands as an indication of their need. Then a prayer for "healing in mass" was offered.

In her story about John Andrew's healing, Mrs. Leali writes, "When Brother BonGiovanni declared, 'In the name of Jesus, be healed,' Claudia felt John Andrew shake in her arms. A tingling sensation leapt from his body to hers.' " Later Claudia also took John forward to be anointed with oil according to James 5:14. Something unusual obviously happened to the little boy.

Mrs. Leali describes it. "From that day on, in gradual stages, John Andrew's head began to return to normal size. The child who at 6 months had lain in a semi-stupor and would not follow a light with his eyes was, at 13 months, able to walk. His growth was accelerated. By the time he was two years of age, the doctors had pronounced him normal."

CHAPTER **12**

The XRay Told A Different Story

The surgeon's office was quite impressive, nicely appointed with furniture, artifacts and honoraria, both earned and awarded, from various institutions and organizations. It was obvious this person was not your ordinary cut of humanity.

The previous week during a regular check-up, my personal physician, Dr. Robert Cicuto, discovered evidence of a polyp in my colon. I was here by his recommendation and appointment.

Dr. William Henwood was direct and to the point in his orientation. A colonoscopy and the surgical removal of the polyp was recommended. The procedure was scheduled at the Farrell Osteopathic Hospital, now known as the Shenango Valley Health Center.

There is always a measure of anxiety in anticipated surgery. But I was confident the attending surgeon was highly qualified. However, we were not prepared for our Lord's surprise.

I was only partially sedated since the procedure didn't require a complete anesthetic. I was aware of all that was happening. And there was a minimal degree of pain and discomfort as Dr. Henwood performed the colonoscopy.

Sometimes even physicians with the most refined skill and sensitivity are baffled at what they find. Or, as in my case, by what they *can't* find! For, search as he would, the good doctor could not locate the polyp earlier seen on my Xray.

I still recall vividly, Dr. Henwood reaching up for the Xray and pulling it down to where I could check it over from my position on the surgical table. "Look," he said to me in frustration, as he held the Xray with his left hand and tapped it where the polyp appeared on it with the back of his right hand, "It's here. But I can't find it!" And he never did.

Something obviously had happened between the taking of the Xray and the time for surgery to remove the polyp pictured in it.

I was relieved and extremely grateful that no cutting was necessary; and we, of course, attributed the "disappearance" of the polyp to a supernatural work of the Lord, Who is our Healer. Although we had prayed for healing in a rather general way, I couldn't recall any special ministry for my healing or any special sense that I had been blest with the Lord's healing virtue. So, I was a bit puzzled by how things happened, although I was indeed grateful for the healing.

As I reflected upon the events preceding surgery, I had to conclude the healing must have taken place during a visit with a Christian businessman from Cleveland, Ohio. I was General Overseer of the Christian Church of North America at the time. Brother Pensa visited in my office in Transfer, PA.

I recalled his prayer as we stood in closing his visit in my office. No reference had been made to my scheduled surgery. But in his prayer, Brother Pensa asked the Lord to bring to me His healing blessing. It was just that simple. And I recall that I was somewhat puzzled, although pleased, that he should pray in such a manner.

It appears that the Lord directed his prayer for the healing of my body. As accurately as I can recall, that's the reason the

Xray told a different story from what the surgeon discovered.

CHAPTER **13**

In a Dream She Saw the Street and House Number

This story involves two women of faith. I didn't have the privilege of knowing Mrs. Germano, personally. From what I have been told, she apparently was a devout woman who experienced the direction of the Lord in unusual ways. But I did know Mrs. De Vito. She was a member of the First Assembly of God (then known as the Farrell Christian Assembly), during the years I served that church as pastor. During my pastoral calls on this quiet, reserved and dedicated woman, I was blessed as she recalled how in earlier years she learned of our church and became a member.

Mrs. DeVito was born and reared in Italy. She was united in marriage in Italy to Mr. DeVito, who had gone to Italy to find a bride. Apparently, Mrs. DeVito had found

Christ as her personal Savior while yet in Italy.

As she traveled by boat to the land of her new husband, Mrs. DeVito was deeply concerned about the cultural changes she was sure to encounter. In her prayers she said, "Lord, please help me. I am going to a strange land, with a strange language. I have no friends there. Please send someone of the Faith to help me." This was her daily prayer.

Not long after she was settled in Farrell, PA., God answered Mrs. DeVito's prayer. As she answered the knock on the door early one morning, she discovered a little Italian woman standing there.

What startled her even more than the early visit was the greeting from this stranger. She raised her hand as if in blessing and in Italian said, "Peace!" Mrs. DeVito instantly recognized the greeting. It was practiced among Born Again believers in her native Italy, and distinguished them as members of the Faith.

A smile burst across her face as special joy exploded inside her. Her awareness that God had answered her prayer was overwhelming. Mrs. DeVito knew a sister-in-the-Lord was at her door!

Instinctively, she responded to the greeting by saying, "Amen," in the typical Italian way. Then she enthusiastically went on to ask, "But how do you know I am a sister?"

Mrs. Germano explained, "Last night in a dream I saw your street. I saw your house. I saw the number on your house. And I saw you. Then God told me to visit you and bring you to the fellowship of God's people in this city." That's all there was to it. But it was impacting enough to motivate Mrs. Germano to rise early and seek out this child of God who felt alone in a strange land.

Many years had intervened from the time of that experience and the moment of retelling it to me. But the powerful impact and delightful joy of knowing God heard Mrs. DeVito's prayers and supernaturally led someone to help her find her way in a strange land, yet radiated from her face. This is an awfully big universe and a lot to command God's attention. But there could be no question in Mrs. DiVito's mind, God knew exactly where she was. She was convinced He was truly concerned about her, personally!

" When thou passest
through the waters,
I will be with thee;
and through the rivers,
they will not overflow thee:
when thou walkest through the fire,
thou shalt not be burned;
neither shall the flame
kindle upon thee....
When the enemy
shall come in like a flood,
the Spirit of the LORD
shall lift up a standard
against him. "
Isaiah 43:2; 59: 19

CHAPTER **14**

Lions Walked Into The Dining Room And The Mafia Hit Men Were Stopped

He was a big, burly man, unlettered and unskilled in speech. But the heart that beat within him was warm with affection and as big as he was. In his size and comportment, more than any other man, he most closely fits my personal perception of Peter the Apostle.

"Pop Chiodo" as we affectionately called him, always felt we had a special kinship. It was a bond each of us enjoyed as much as the other. As a matter of fact, it was he who reminded the board of the Farrell church of me when they sat down to call a successor to the Rev. Peter Bonafiglia. But his sense of kinship reached to my personal roots.

I was born in Sagamore, a little coal mining town in Western Pennsylvania. (When I was three months of age, I'm told the family relocated to the nearby town of Dayton, in Armstrong County.) Pop Chiodo was also from this region, and that brought a unique identification to us both.

While living in Sagamore, Pop's reputation quickly spread as a crack marksman with a revolver. Even in his later years, when I came to know him, I witnessed he had not lost his skill with a revolver. He was able to shoot down empty shell cases set up as targets at a considerable distance.

Pop's ability quickly came to the attention of an active Mafia. He had the kind of skill they liked to recruit. And in time, an attempt was made to recruit him as one of their "hit men." Although not as yet a Christian, Pop was a moral and a caring man. He respectfully declined, knowing his refusal now made him a "marked" man. Within a short time, to protect himself and his family, Pop relocated to a home in Sharon, Pennsylvania. As I visited with him in that very home one day, he told me of the Mafia's attempt to eliminate him and how God spared him by a supernatural demonstration of His power.

Pop had always been a devout man. As a Roman Catholic, he cared for the statuary and served in other ways in St. Anthony's church, just across the street from his home in Sharon. His devotion to God only intensified now that he had become a "Born Again" evangelical. And it was his practice to give himself quite extensively to prayer, especially since the passing of his wife.

One summer afternoon while kneeling at prayer in his Dining Room, the large French doors between the Living Room and the Dining Room, slowly opened. There -to use his description- stood " a tall skinny man and a short, little man chewing on a cigar. "

Startled by the appearance of the men, Pop rose from his knees and asked, "Who are you?"

"We are members of the Mafia from Sagamore," they responded.

"What do you want with me?" Pop continued.

"We've come to kill you."

Pop was startled at their response. "Why do you want to do that?"

They explained. "Because you know who we are."

"But I'm not gonna tell anybody," Pop pleaded with them. "Your secret is safe with me." But his words fell on deaf ears. They moved in, preparing to snuff out the life of this man of God.

Then the unexpected happened! "Suddenly," Pop said to me, " It looked like the blood left their faces. They got white — real white — like they had no blood." He continued with deepening emotion now, "And then they turned around, quick, and ran out of the Dining Room. They ran down the stairs and out of the house from the basement door where they broke in. I never saw them again! They were gone." Pop was dazed by what happened, but grateful that his life was spared.

Three years passed. One day, Pop routinely answered the knock on his front door. When he opened it, he was startled to discover one of those Mafia men had returned. (I can't recall whether the tall or short one.)

Quickly the man assured Pop he had come in peace and intended no harm. He told Pop he had come actually to ask his forgiveness for the attempt on Pop's life three years earlier. He further shared with Pop the welcome news that he had accepted Christ as his personal Savior. He was, himself, no longer associated with the Mafia.

As they sat chatting in the very room where three years earlier this man had attempted to kill Pop, he finally asked a question that had troubled him from the day he ran out of the Chiodo home in fear.

"Tell me, Brother," said the former Mafioso, "where did you get those two big lions that were in your house that day?"

"What two lions, " asked a puzzled Mr. Chiodo, "I don't got no lions!"

The man explained. "As we moved toward you, two lions walked into the room and stood alongside of you, one on one side and another on the other side."

Pop Chiodo, of course owned no lions. He probably didn't even own a cat! He and his visitor were obligated to conclude that what had occurred was a demonstration of God's supernatural power. It seemed quite obvious the appearance of angelic, beings in the form of lions, materialized before the eyes of committed assassins in order to protect the man of God.

Some years later I shared Pop's experience with the congregation during a Sunday afternoon Camp Meeting in Sharpsville, Pennsylvania. After the service a young man introduced himself to me. To this day, I regret I failed to get his name! He told me he knew about the attempt on Pop's life, and the way the lions had protected him. He wanted to confirm to me that what Pop had told me was true. He could verify it because one of the two men who made an attempt on Pop's life, the one who later came to ask forgiveness of Pop, was his uncle!

Addendum:

At a church dinner in Northeast Ohio, while standing in an informal circle of friends, I was sharing this story when a gentleman, who was listening attentively suddenly broke into my comments and said, "I know that story."
I was puzzled. " Did you hear me tell it from the pulpit?"
He nodded his head, no.
"Did you read it in my book?"
Again, he nodded, no.
"So, where did you learn of it?" I again asked.
With a mischievous twinkle in his eyes, the man who in his preconversion days apparently had some dubious connections in a large nearby city said, "I heard about it years ago in....," naming the city he came from.
What an amazing development of events to learn the news of Pop Chiodo's extraordinary experience had traveled through the Mafia "network" all the way from Sagamore, PA to a large eastern Ohio city and reached the ear of this gentleman, who now many years later, bears witness to the authenticity of this supernatural intervention.

CHAPTER **15**

When God Scuttled A Special Business Meeting Of A Church Denomination

When one carefully examines the disappointments in life, he must conclude that over the long term, they are, in reality, *re*appointments orchestrated by the Lord. Of course, the Lord does not bring to us painful experiences. He leads us out of them within His own time-frame; and carefully sees to it that some good emerges, even from the worst scenario. New relationships, new vocations, new skills, new strength are the frequent fruit of such frustration. Esther and I have had our share, and we know our Lord's faithfulness.

One of our earliest disappointments was destined to change the course of our lives. It made it possible for us to accept a pastorate we didn't even know was available at the time of the disappointment. I had been asked to consider serving as a full-time Youth Leader by the Overseer of what was known in 1956 as the Eastern District of the Christian Church of North America. We saw the need and were happy to accept the challenge. It would be a new experience for us, and for the District.

Because it was ultimately the local pastors with whom I would have to work, I did insist, however, that my appointment would be ratified by the District Ministerium. For that purpose, Rev. Gaetano Bavaro, pastor of Esther's home church and secretary-treasurer of the District, informed us a special session of the District had been scheduled. At the time the meeting was to convene, I was in revival meetings with the Rev. Vito Tedesco in Tacony, PA. So, I personally could not be present.

Upon my return to the Bronx from Tacony, one of the first things I did was to telephone Brother Bavaro about the ratification. He was apologetic, and somewhat puzzled as he explained. For some reason, in their pre-business session conference, the Presbytery became so enmeshed in concerns about providing training for pastors, that issue spilled over into the business session; and they just didn't get to the primary purpose for calling the special Business Session! It was an unusual twist of circumstances.

I explained to the Secretary that I needed to get on with my life; that out of concern for my family, we could not afford to wait for some future determination by Council, and respectfully asked to be released from my commitment to the District. He understood, and we moved on.

Of course, we were disappointed, but it wasn't the first time. In the Spring of that year, several months earlier, a national officer of the denomination asked us to develop a budget that would make it possible for us to travel as tent evangelists for the Movement. We did so enthusiastically and happily.

During a casual contact with that officer some time later, however, both Esther and I sensed considerable indifference about the tent ministry. Over the Labor Day weekend, at the annual convention of the Movement, convened at Pine Grove Camp in Malaga, N.J., we were to learn why.

We sat in disbelief as we listened to this man give an enthusiastic report about the tent ministry, the cities where it had been, the preachers who led the meetings.

When we talked with him later, he casually dismissed our reminder that he had engaged us to work out a budget and ministry plan for the tent. And even as he later presented us to the convention, along with other young ministers, his introductory comments about us were quite anemic by comparison with others. So much so, that it caught the attention of an elderly pastor, whose church I would eventually serve.

We were disappointed and disillusioned at the leader's insensitivity. In retrospect, however, we now can see that those disappointments actually contributed to making a new and exciting ministry possible for us. But, at the time, it hurt. It really hurt.

During my services in Tacony, Esther and the baby stayed with her family in the Bronx. In those days meetings customarily were held for one or two weeks, with a Monday and sometimes Saturday off. One Monday it was possible for me to drive the few hours to the Bronx to be with my family.

That evening Esther and I drove out to our former apartment to pick up the mail. We were surprised and pleased to find waiting for us a letter from the Board of the church served by Brother Peter Bonafiglia. He was the elderly pastor who caught the contrast in the introductory comments during the convention in Malaga. The Board wanted to know if we were interested in pastoral ministry; specifically, in Farrell, PA.

Esther and I quickly realized a supernatural power had prevented her from picking up the mail at the apartment while I was in Tacony. The letter from Farrell was in our apartment mailbox for a full week! That was way out of character from our normal way of doing things. But, had she picked up the letter, she would have informed me of it by telephone and I would have been obligated to decline the invitation. I was already committed to the Eastern District youth position, and I had been assured ratification by the ministerium was a mere formality. We actually received the Farrell letter only after Brother Bavaro released us from our commitment to the Eastern District.

It's amazing — and humbling — to me to realize God apparently *detoured* a special District business session and prevented Esther from picking up our mail for a full week, in order for us to accept the call to the Farrell church. Intelligent people know the possibilities of this happening *coincidentally* are quite remote. Somebody clearly orchestrated the events that brought us to the pulpit of the Farrell Christian Assembly.

*" Give,
and it shall be given
unto you;
good measure,
pressed down,
and shaken together,
and running over,
shall men give
into your bosom.
For with the same measure
that ye mete withal
it shall be measured
to you again. "*
Luke 6:38

CHAPTER **16**

The Mystery Of Giving Money You Don't Have, From Sources You Don't Know About

Shortly after assuming pastoral duties in Farrell, God began to make it clear to me that He is, Himself, the Source of the money needed to accomplish His purposes; and that an understanding of the patterns and laws governing His blessing is openly available in the Scripture. My studies led me to discover "The Covenant of Blessing" through which a tithing church was developed, permitting us to erect a modern church plant as well as support the local ministries of the church without fiscal stress.

The Covenant of Blessing

This all occurred at the peak of an economic recession. But we aggressively prayed for employment on the basis of "The Covenant of Blessing," actually with the laying on of hands upon our men who lost their jobs.

I recall one Sunday evening in particular when we offered prayer for two of our men who reported loss of employment. The people believed God with our Brethren in need. And we were not disappointed.

During the next Wednesday evening service, Phil Davano testified to the congregation, "Since Sunday night I was offered, not just one, but three jobs."

James Sylvester immediately followed him by saying, "This is going to sound funny. But the same thing happened to me!" And why not? God is no respector of persons.

During that recession, in one of our city churches comparable in size to the Farrell Christian Assembly, we were informed 50 families lost their jobs and were without income. But not one family in our church, to our knowledge, suffered without steady income. Our men lost jobs, but we prayed them through to new employment or entrepreneural income. We believe "The Covenant of Blessing" and aggressive prayer made the difference.

The Faith Promise

Not long into the ministry in Farrell, the Lord began to help me realize that although I was active in missions, in reality I had no personal method for giving to missions. Of course, we scheduled missionaries. And we dropped our offerings in the basket like everybody else. But I sensed something definitely was missing. My search for the missing ingredient led me to the discovery of the Faith Promise, a concept of giving pioneered by the missionary statesman, Oswald J. Smith.

The Faith Promise was distinct from and in addition to the Tithe, which was the monetary dimension of "The Covenant of Blessing." The latter is based upon one's "increase" and is intended to assure sufficient resources to support the local ministry of the church.

The Faith Promise is a partnership with God, through which one trusts the Lord to provide for missions -beyond the local church- monies he doesn't have from sources he doesn't know about. It is based exclusively upon one's personal conviction that God wants him to believe a specific amount of money will be supplied to him for missions, either through unexpected sources or through ideas for income which he can implement.

In any event, giving is elevated from strictly an economic consideration to a concern of faith. "According to your faith, be it unto you" (Matt. 9:29). The Lord communicates the dollar amount. We trust Him to supply it. Then we give it for missions. In no case is it to be taken out of savings or current resources, excepting of course, those funds are in excess of what they should be and the Lord makes it clear an "adjustment" in one's living budget should be made.

It was an exciting discovery and the series of Missions Conventions, at the heart of which was the Faith Promise, were productive beyond imagination. A few years later, having assumed the position of Director of Missions, I was able to introduce the Faith Promise to the General Council, Christian Church of North America. To suggest it was revolutionary would be an understatement. It wasn't only that giving to missions skyrocketed by over 600%. The more important impact was in the numbers of people motivated in the total missionary enterprise. A dynamic was released that built upon the base established by my esteemed predecessor, the Rev. R.L. Corsini, that continues to this day.

Two Gold Coins

Immediately following one of our local missions conventions, Julie Martino, an unusually devout Christian, shared a struggle she faced with her Faith Promise. The amount she sensed the Lord was leading her to trust Him for was so large she needed reassurance.

With hesitation she finally said she believed the Lord was asking her to trust Him to supply through her $1,000 for missions. As I think back on her circumstances, I can understand her reticence. She had no job. She had four children to care for. Her husband was a hard working man. But their income certainly was not lavish. It was a real challenge!

We talked a bit and prayed, committing the matter to the Lord. If, indeed, it was of Him, He would supply it; if not, there was no damage done. It would be a learning experience either way, I assured her.

Months passed and nothing happened. Occasionally we talked about it, reaffirming our trust in the Lord. We always encouraged the people to be in touch with us if their Faith Promise was in trouble. Julie was not the kind of woman who casually made commitments and just as casually walked away from them. Julie was real, and the relationship with her Lord must be real.

Not much time remained before the subsequent Missions Convention. All the monies we had been trusting God to supply for missions must be in before that. Julie knew that, and she prayed even more intensely. Had she misunderstood the Lord's direction? Was something wrong? She wrestled with all the normal questions.

Then, her aged grandfather was hospitalized. He soon passed on and his will was read. To her amazement, Grandpa had left her two gold coins! Her husband quickly — and understandably— thought of the children's shoes and clothing needed for the next school year. There also were some repairs needed on their house. But Julie immediately realized, this must be the way the Lord would supply the money for the Faith Promise she was led to write nearly 12 months earlier.

Upon receiving the coins, Julie immediately had their value appraised. Julie listened intently. The jeweler said, "$1,000." The exact amount she was led to trust God for a year ago! Her heart leaped for joy, not only because of what this amount could do in world evangelization, but also because it confirmed to her that she, indeed, had been led of the Lord. But the challenge was not over.

As Julie and her husband discussed their new resource, with appropriate caution her husband pointed out the existing needs in their own family. Perhaps they should consider these needs, too. They were real, not imaginary —or extravagant. It's a continuing tribute to their devotion and faith that husband and wife, both committed to the higher will of God, and to the needs of others.

The $1,000 Julie believed for and which the Lord supplied was given for missions.

The Honey Bees

Several months following one of our Missions Conventions, I walked into the employee entrance of the Leali Brothers Meat Processing Plant in Wheatland, PA. Standing directly in the line of my entry was Paul, one of the five Leali brothers who were rapidly making their mark in our Valley as successful businessmen.

Paul was *planted* there. It seemed like he knew ahead of time exactly when I would open that door. He didn't say anything. He just stood there staring at me. His hands were jammed into his trouser pockets. I would say he was in the military "at ease" position, except he was anything but at ease!

Paul gave no greeting. He wasn't angry. But he had something definitely on his mind. As I closed the distance between us he spoke up. "Those bees are costing me more money than what they're worth!"

I knew what he was talking about. I always encouraged our congregation to ask God for "Ideas for Income" on which to base their Faith Promise. Paul took the suggestion, and believing the Lord was leading him to do so, registered a sizable Faith Promise on the idea that he could harvest enough honey from his bee hives to cover the total amount.

"I've had to dump more sugar into those hives than what they're worth," he continued. Then in his inimitable way, he explained, "Now don't misunderstand! It's not that I can't sit down and write a check for the total amount. I can do that. But that wasn't the deal!"

He paused a moment as if to collect his thoughts, still in the "at ease" position with hands jammed into his pockets. "Now I figure it this way. He knows better than I do if He needs it. If the bees produce honey, I give it. If not, there's nothing to give!"

Anyone who understands Paul knows he wasn't being arrogant or disrespectful of me or of the Lord. Paul is one of the most direct persons I know. He just tells it like it is.

Then he went to "closure." "You told us if we get in trouble with our Faith Promise to tell you; so, I'm telling you. I figure you have a better connection than I do."

Paul was right. Not about the connection, I told him, but in telling me how his faith was being tested. I encouraged him to keep trusting God, and to agree with me that the Lord would come through on his Faith Promise.

Finishing my visit with the men, I quickly drove to my study, fell to my knees and earnestly asked the Lord to not let this man's faith be frustrated. I had no further contact with Paul for about three weeks.

When I walked in the Plant about three weeks later, Paul greeted me with a big smile. " I don't know what you did, but it sure is working! My bees are bringing in so much honey, now I'm having a time keeping up with them adding layers to the hives!"

Quite obviously, something very unusual happened. In a season during which, I was told, most of the bee keepers in Mercer County "starved," Paul had a hard time keeping up with his hard working bees. The big difference could well be, Paul's bees were working for missions!

*" I have learned,
in whatsoever state I am,
therewith to be content.
I know both how to be abased,
and I know how to abound:
every where and in all things
I am instructed both to be full
and to be hungry,
both to abound
and to suffer need.
I can do all things
through Christ
which strengtheneth me
by Christ Jesus."*
Philippians 4:11-13, 19

CHAPTER **17**

How To Build A Home With No Money for a Down Payment; Yet, Have Enough Left Over To Buy a Printing Plant!

The title of this chapter is rhetorically designed to capture your attention. Of course, it didn't happen exactly that way. *Sequence* and *timing* are the missing ingredients. The statement becomes true only as you learn the printing plant was purchased several years after our house was built; and that the equity in the house — even though meager at that time — became leverage for purchasing the Plant. It was a *big* part of the miracle. Without the equity the purchase could not have been made.

Purchasing the Plant represents a series of events that reflect much more than mere human ingenuity. One of my colleagues, who recognized the natural unlikelihood of such a purchase, telephoned after reading about it in the paper to ask, "Hey, Guy, how does one buy a printing plant on a preacher's salary?" My response, of course, was a tribute to the Lord.

I mention the building of our house in this book because it is, of itself, an exciting series of events illustrating our Lord's miraculous provision. But, specifically, in the unfolding drama of my life it was pivotal. Without the home, two elements crucial in my life and ministry, would have been impossible:

1.) Owning our own house made it possible for us to accept the directorship for missions with the Christian Church of North America. The salary scale of $100 per week at that time, certainly could not provide living expenses and housing for a family of four; and,

2) Owning our home made it possible to purchase the printing plant. Through it, we were able to provide, at less than commercial rates, materials the Movement desperately needed. At the same time, in God's Providence, the printing business also turned out to be our retirement program. The Movement couldn't do it; so the Lord graciously arranged a private plan for us.

The Key Person

Ralph Perilli, who was a member of the Farrell Christian Assembly and a salesman for Keystone Homes, became the key person the Lord would use to provide leadership for us to build our house. At the time, we didn't have "two nickels to rub together," and negotiating a loan was out of the question.

The firm Ralph represented had a special provision for people in our situation. If a couple owned property on which to build, Ralph's company would build the home and arrange a thirty year mortgage. No down payment was needed! Not only that. Ralph graciously offered his commission as a contribution to our home, in addition to the leadership he would provide. But I needed land.

A Gift of Land

That's when Dan Leali stepped forward — quiet, unpretentious, but purposeful. He wanted to *give* us land, almost an acre! I had been his pastor for several years and followed him with our concern and prayers though his youth, during his dangerous military service in Beirut and now in his business ventures.

Dan was known more for his works than for his words. He didn't say much, but he had a generous heart. So, it was not out of character for him to offer the land free of charge.

I reminded Dan of some Scriptures as I turned down his gracious offer. "The laborer is worthy of his hire....thou shalt not muzzle the ox that treadeth out the corn" (Luke 10:7; 1 Corinthians 9:9). I explained he had worked hard to get the land. He should get at least some benefit from it. If he wanted to discount the land, I would concede to it with deep appreciation. But I didn't think I should get the land without cost from a man who earned it "by the sweat of his brow."

It was done. But a new problem would soon emerge.

An Interest-free Loan

At my request, a subcommittee of the church Board cost-analyzed the out-of-pocket cash required of the church to maintain our parsonage. It was my recommendation the church add that amount to my salary —what it *already was paying out to others* to maintain a parsonage—, and I would see to my own housing. It would cost the church nothing more than what it was currently paying. In addition, I suggested receipts from the sale of the parsonage should be put against the church mortgage. The ten thousand dollars we expected from the sale would go a long way toward reducing the church's monthly mortgage payments. It was a win-win situation.

The subcommittee's report was more than we expected. It not only recommended selling the parsonage and increasing my salary by the amount the church had been paying for its upkeep. They went a step further. Rather than put money from the sale against the church mortgage, the Committee recommended it should be offered to me and Esther as an interest-free loan to help us build our home. The full Board, and later by resolution, the congregation, quickly approved the arrangement. It was a heart warming gesture by a congregation Esther and I by that time had served ten years.

With it, a new scenario emerged. We were no longer limited to the Keystone Homes plan. With the church loan, we could now negotiate a conventional loan on a different kind of home. It was exciting!

A Rental
At the time we certainly weren't in a seller's market. Nevertheless, the parsonage sold within good time. The buyer wanted to get in, and of course, we had to get out. But we had no place to go! Over the previous ten years, we had moved several times within our church area. But each time, we knew where we were going. This time it was different.

Every effort, either of the Board or our own, was unsuccessful. There just were no places to rent! Of course, we were in constant prayer, both personally and as a congregation. I had personally telephoned every realtor in our Valley for a rental. None was available. It was the kind of situation in which everyone is keenly aware that God must intervene. And He did!

One of those quiet members of our church, Mary DeFazio, learned that a neighbor was about to rent his house in Wheatland. She telephoned and learned we just missed it! But all was not lost. He had just made a verbal commitment to rent. No lease had been signed, however, and the renter had been told the home would be held for him only until 9:30 that evening. After that, he would feel free to rent to others. Mary telephoned us with the information.

We kept the matter before the Lord, asking Him to delay or detour the other renter if it was His will that we live in Wheatland. For several hours we prayed, and watched the clock! Shortly after 9:30, we learned the other renter hadn't showed up, and the house was ours.

A few days after we had taken residence in Wheatland, the buyer of the parsonage came by to pick up some keys. He marveled at our house. Indeed, it was an excellent little ranch house in very good condition. He said he had scoured the Valley for a rental unit —as I had— without success. His original intention as a newly wed was to rent, rather than buy. Then he asked how we located the house. We simply told him our story. We believe it was an act of God!

Now that things were coming together, Esther and I scoured the parsonage looking for a book of house plans we bought one evening many years earlier. A picture of our dream home was on the cover.

At the time, we knew possibilities of ever building it —or any home, for that matter —were extremely remote. In fact, like most minister's wives living on a limited income, Esther felt we would never own our own home. Eventually, we located the book, sent for the plans and were ready to go, except....

The bank wanted a clear deed on the land, and we didn't have the $500 needed to clear it. That's when another miracle happened through the quiet man with a big heart.

Without a word to us, Dan put $500 of his own money through the bank in my name to get a clear deed —and gave it to us! We were speechless as he turned to leave saying,

"Pay when you can. No hurry." And he meant it!

He Threw the Check at Her!

A few months after we were in our new house, we sent Dan a check for $25.00. We felt we had to make at least some gesture of our intention to return the money. We didn't want to abuse our Brother's kindness.

A few days later, Esther answered the door bell. It was Dan. He didn't say, "Hello," or "How are you?" or anything. He just threw the check at her! Then asked, "Who's pushing you?" That was it!

Esther did her best to explain our gratitude and our concern. We didn't want to abuse his kindness. But he reminded her, "There's no hurry." It was not that he had money to spare. As a young man just out of military service and starting out in business, we knew he didn't. It was just the kind of caring attitude among our church family that made our house possible, and the ministries that later would be possible because of it.

Ralph Perilli orchestrated a chain of miracles. Jim Calvert, a fine Christian gentleman and owner of Calvert Lumber Company in Sharon, PA. would provide all the building supplies virtually at his cost. Joe Chiodo picked up bricks with his truck at an Ohio brickyard; then did the brick work on the house. His brother, Toire, did the roofing and gutters with his son, Anthony. John Marcucci helped me drill holes and string the wire throughout the house, and John Apa, Jr. connected all the electrical wires as they should be. Several of the men helped me put up the plaster board. John Benigas, Glen Gigliotti and John Marcucci put in the sidewalk. And one summer day, 69 baby pines were planted by the Men's Fellowship around the perimeter of our property, just before a good rain.

All of these Brethren contributed their services, and they have our undying gratitude. But more importantly, they share, both here and hereafter, in the blessing that is assured those who are fellow helpers of those whom the Lord calls into His service.

Urie Byler, a fine, young Amish builder, did the major construction. He did a superb job although he had never before built a split level house. And he built it at a rate reduced from his already low cost. Such kindness will not go unnoticed by our Lord.

"Mommy! Is this a palace?
A newly constructed house, however, needs carpeting and furniture. And the Lord hadn't overlooked that either! Esther and I were looking around our new house on a beautiful day soon after it was under roof. As we stood in the living room area, a young

man poked his head in the doorway and introduced himself. We chatted a while, then he said, "Reverend, I'd like to do your interior decorating for you." That was appealing, but I thought impossible.

"I'd like for you to do it, too, but I can't afford it."

Charlie made his offer. In exchange for using our home for referrals, he would do the carpeting and furniture at his cost, plus a small markup to cover some of his overhead. In this way we could get the best custom made furniture and Charlie's expertise at a cost no greater than what we would have to pay to buy it off the floor in a furniture store. We were pleased with the offer and recognized again the hand of the Lord in it.

One of the highest compliments to Charlie's expertise came from a child. While visiting in our home with her parents one evening, she asked her Mother, "Mommy, is this a palace?"

That working relationship allowed a friendship to develop with Charlie and his wife Lynn. Referrals from it also nurtured their fledgling business. And we like to feel it contributed in some way to what today is recognized as a major furniture establishment in the Shenango Valley, Knott's Interiors.

Getting the Reverend "Out of the mud"

A particularly moving provision of the Lord came through Benjamin Gibbs. Ben was an active member of the Cedar Avenue Church of God, and a fine gentleman. He and his wife regularly attended our three-evening Couples' Clinics at the church.

We had been living in our new house for a few months when Ben stopped by to chat with me. Unfortunately, I was not home. But he told my wife to tell me he was "going to get me out of the mud." He was referring to our unfinished driveway. Since he owned a paving company, he had the ability to do it. He made it clear he also had the heart for it.

That weekend, at Ben's request, I offered prayer at the dedication ceremony of a swimming pool that was a primary phase of a children's camp Ben was developing. While chatting with him after the ceremony, I asked Ben what it would cost me for him to "get me out of the mud."

His response was immediate and firm, "Reverend, when I say I'm going to get you out of the mud, I'm going to get you out of the mud!" And closing his eyes while spreading his arms like an umpire calling a player out, he quickly followed up by saying, "It's not going to cost you a dime!" I couldn't believe my ears.

"Ben, I can't let you do that. It's a long driveway." He wouldn't hear it. "Well, let me at least cover the cost of your materials and workers," I pleaded. There was no changing his mind.

Bright and early one Friday morning, the Gibbs Paving Company crew and equipment arrived. They labored all day. I told a friend, it looked like he was putting in a highway! Ben wanted to make sure the driveway would last. And it has! At this writing, some 25 years later, apart from a couple applications of sealer contributed by the Carman Davano and Pantalone Paving Companies, it hasn't required any repairs.

As his men were finishing for the day, Ben sauntered over to me and asked who would be doing the finished grading around the house. I chuckled as I told him, "Ben, I haven't even thought that far yet."

"I'll be over in the morning to do it," he said. And next day, he and one of his employees pushed dirt around for hours until all the unsightly mounds of dirt were leveled and the grade complemented the house well, leaving only the planting of grass to complete the job.

And to our amazement, on our return from preaching a Camp Meeting, we discovered several men of the church finished that task, too!

It would be an understatement of gigantic proportions to simply say we were and continue to be overwhelmed at the good favor of the Lord, and the willingness of so many dear friends to be His instruments in helping provide a home that in the future was destined to facilitate such a broadening of our ministry that people in six continents would be reached with the Gospel of Christ. The future destiny of what was happening in the building of our house was imperceptible, but the chain of miracles was quite obvious as they unfolded.

> *" Therefore I say unto you,*
> *Take no thought for your life,*
> *what ye shall eat,*
> *or what ye shall drink;*
> *nor yet for your body,*
> *what ye shall put on.*
> *Is not the life more than meat,*
> *and the body than raiment?*
> *Behold the fowls of the air:*
> *for they sow not,*
> *neither do they reap,*
> *nor gather into barns;*
> *yet your heavenly Father feedeth them.*
> *Are ye not much better than they?.*
> *...But seek ye first the kingdom of God,*
> *and his righteousness;*
> *and all these things shall be added unto you."*
> Matthew 6:25,26,33

CHAPTER **18**

The Key To Purchasing A Printing Company On A Pastor's Salary

From my earliest days I've had a keen interest in literature and its related fields. I was class editor and later editor-in-chief of the Eastern Bible Institute (now Valley Forge Christian College) yearbook, "Vision." Mary Abate Corvine, a dear friend who was an evangelist at the time, picked-up on my youthful interest and in her unique manner encouraged me by saying, "One day you will publish your own magazine." Whether or not she spoke prophetically I can't say. But I never forgot her comment.

As things developed through the years, with the help of the Dominick Tedesco family, who owned a printing plant in Erie, Pennsylvania, it was my pleasure to publish a number of small books and "Christianity," a magazine of applied Christian truth. Later, through our own plant, we published for the secular market, "Dine 'N Do" magazine, with an estimated readership of 80,000 in Northwestern Pennsylvania and Northeastern Ohio. For several years, I also did the editorial and graphic design work for "Power" magazine, the full color magazine of the R.W. Schambach Ministries, distributed to over 300,000 people monthly.

These and other publications have brought satisfaction and fulfillment of vision, of course. But the most significant event in my relationship to publications —and later to be seen as another evidence of our Lord's gracious provision— was the purchase of a printing plant of historic significance.

The timing of the opportunity to purchase the plant was particularly surprising. As a matter of fact, I was at the moment, selling-off what printing equipment I had! I was already occupied as Executive Director of Missions for The General Council, Christian Church of North America. And although the equipment was useful in providing printed materials for the CCNA, coordinating its use after office hours, became too cumbersome with my other responsibilities; particularly traveling as much as I did. I had to get rid of the "hobby!"

During the process of selling equipment, a friend, who knew of my interest in publications, stopped by my office. Rather casually he said, "Guy, the Globe Printing Company in New Wilmington is up for sale. I thought you might be interested." I thanked him for his thoughtfulness and told him I was, at the moment in fact, selling off the equipment I had. I followed up by remarking quite indifferently that I didn't even know there was a printing plant in New Wilmington. Nothing more was said.

When I needed to place an order for a brochure several weeks later, I suddenly remembered New Wilmington! More out of curiosity about the plant I hadn't know about, than out of serious interest to purchase, I found myself driving to the quaint village, just 9 miles to the South.

As we finished with the details of the order I placed with Chris Hernly, the owner, I casually remarked, "I hear this place is up for sale." What happened next stunned me, to say the least. Mr. Hernley grabbed my wrist, pulled me around the counter and said, "Let me show you around."

I really didn't have an option! But it was okay because I was interested in printing; and I would later learn the reason for Chris' abrupt response.

It was an efficient, well kept and supervised plant. In addition to the usual commercial work, the Company published a weekly newspaper called, "The Globe." The newspaper had been published continuously, every week without fail, since 1880 –a remarkable tribute to the stability of the firm! As such, it was an historical institution, of sorts, of the community. Every week the Company also produced legal journals for the Bar Associations of four counties. Five or six full time and a few part-time people were employed. The potential of the plant was apparent.

It became even more apparant with a later review of the ledgers and Mr. Hernley's offer to supervise the plant until a capable manager could be located and hired. Mr. Hernley, who was not particularly known in the community for his "flexibility," further impressed us with the concessions he offered to make our purchase possible.

After all, we were not investors with a pocket full of money, looking for a place to turn a good profit. All we had to our name was our rather recently built home, and we were "partners" with the bank in that! But precisely here is where, once again, we witnessed our Lord's Providential orchestration of events for our good.

Although we hadn't owned our home for long, there was enough equity in it for us to borrow the down payment required by Mr. Hernley. He "held the paper" on the balance, and monthly payments were arranged that could be covered easily by the operation of the plant. It was a good deal. One might say, it was "made in Heaven!"

The "Heavenly" nature of the purchase became quite apparent as Mr. Hernley and I drove toward the Attorney's office for closing the transaction. Chris, who had a Mennonite background, took the initiative. He said, "Guy, I'm going to tell you now why I'm selling the plant to you." I was all ears!

There was an obvious serenity in his demeanor as he explained. "I'm not particularly a religious man," he confessed. "But, I do pray." He paused a moment, then went on, "When 'Bea' (a reference to his wife, Beatrice) and I learned we had to sell the plant because of my by-pass surgery, we both prayed and asked God to send us a man who loved God and loved printing." Another pause, and then with noticible conviction, he concluded, "When you walked in the plant that day, both 'Bea' and I knew that you were the man."

The "Big Amen!"
The impact of that comment thundered inside me like a giant "Amen!" from Heaven.

It was an unforgetable statement of affirmation. I needed it for reassurance as we faced the biggest acquisition of our lives, and the long term commitment it represented. As a young couple, we were risking virtually everything we had in this new venture. It was, indeed, a word in season! And there would be a few times in the future when the "Big Amen" would serve as a steadying anchor in a stormy sea.

For seventeen years we regarded our ownership of the plant as a stewardship for the Lord. With the passing years, by plowing all the monies it generated back into the operation, we were able to upgrade to computerized state-of-the-art equipment in all departments and develop into the best equipped plant for publications in our area. A closely knit team of 13 full and part-time employees produced quality single and four color process products, eventually aggregating at least five times more than the annual gross when we purchased. And this was as an absentee owner! It was clearly evidence of the Lord's favor.

Whether businessmen recognize it or not, the Bible says the power to get wealth is a gift of the Lord (Deuteronomy 8:18). It takes more than human genius. We knew that, and we could see it operate in the plant.

I vividly recall one summer when our production level exceeded that of our competitors by so much that two paper salesmen remarked to our manager, "Somebody here must know somebody." With a twinkle in his eye, Wayne Carper, who served as our manager at the time and was well acquainted with our commitment to the Lord, simply responded, "Yea, I guess you could say that."

A Good "Retirement"

Yet, our Lord's favor was to be seen even more dramatically in "retirement." Of course, it didn't happen without work and occasions of frustration. The frustration level rises rather sharply, especially when one sees what needs to be done and can be done, but can't do anything about it because of prior claims on his time and talent. That's not unusual, just a fact of life for absentee owners.

Often, through the years, particularly when things got a bit stressed, Esther and I rekindled our waning energies by reminding ourselves, the plant was the Lord's provision for our retirement. We realized we must be good stewards of it. We couldn't forget we actually were trying to get out of a printing *hobby*, when suddenly we were plunged into the printing *business!* We didn't understand the reason for it then. But God did! And slowly the Lord's purpose dawned upon us.

Had He not cared for us so diligently, things would be radically different for us today.

We can identify with the Apostle, who assured the Philippians, "But my God shall supply all your need according to his riches in glory by Christ Jesus" (Philippians 4:19). Our Lord, Himself, declared if Christians "seek first the kingdom of God, and his righteousness; all these things (material things we need) shall be added (provided for them)" (Matthew 6:33).

It was the Lord Who orchestrated all the circumstances that led to the decision and ability to purchase the printing plant. We just followed His leadership! It might strike one as simplistic, but that's one of the major keys to success in any enterprise.

CHAPTER **19**

How To Sell A Business in A Distressed Economy

In July of 1992, Esther and I sold our printing business. Seventeen years earlier, when we were getting *out* of a printing *hobby,* through some very unusual circumstances, the Lord reversed our course and put us *into* the printing *business!* Through all those years, the knowledge that *God* put us in the business helped us weather the inevitable ups and downs of business. And selling the plant was never a serious consideration.

A Stewardship From the Lord

The Plant was so clearly a gift of the Lord, we dared not *initiate* selling the business without His clear direction, even though we did sense the time was near just before we were released to sell.

It was during prayer one night in mid March, I sensed a strong release to place the sale of the Plant before the Lord. It was the Lord's prodding. I hadn't asked for the Globe Printing Company. The Lord put it in my charge, and I wasn't about to take any kind of action to change that without His clear direction! Given those circumstances, if it really was the Lord's time, I made it clear to Him, *He* would have to provide a buyer, *miraculously.*

Not Even My Wife Knew

It was amazing! No one knew of my talk with the Lord, not even my wife. There was neither private nor public advertising. But things moved rapidly. In just four days, a total stranger from Cleveland, Ohio telephoned. He wanted to come and talk about buying the business. A week later a man from our community approached me about renting office space. Then, he suddenly asked, "Are you interested in selling the place?"

"Why do you ask?"

"If you're interested in selling, I'd like to buy it. I'm sure I could get the financing."

Several days after that, a close friend made offer number three, and another represented number four. Yet another week and offer number five came in from a graphic supply salesman who moved into our community a year earlier. And nobody had told any of these prospective buyers about my interest in selling!

Frustrated Priorities

When my friend Richard Stienlechner made his offer, I suppose I was on the edge of a pity party. He was aware I, personally, had been managing the revitalization of the Plant since the first of the year. One thing was sure: I was tired...very, very tired! But he listened patiently as I complained. "I like printing," I remarked. "But God called me to preach, not print!"

I had been an absentee owner for seventeen years while I served as an officer in my denomination. Because Esther traveled with me, we had to depend upon the expertise and commitment of managers. Some worked out well, some not so well. Unfortunately, in the three years before we sold, the business had slipped into an unprecedented downturn. Clients had been disenfranchised. Creditors became impatient. That's part of the price for being an absentee owner!

To stay afloat, we re-mortgaged our home and lived off our savings. We had no other income. Some choice long term employees had to be laid off, people whom we regarded more as family than as employees. It was not a pleasant time for us. But they understood and the transition went well. To conserve funds, Esther and I assumed every task in the Plant we could handle, from cleaning rest rooms to calling on clients.

Dick knew better than anyone the pressure we had been under. Our friendship dated back to the early '70s, when both of us were somewhat in the beginnings of our business ventures. By now, he had successfully established more than one business, including Protective Security Systems, which monitors client security businesses across the nation. We especially valued his insights. In fact, at the time, he was installing a more efficient computerized accounting system for us.

As we chatted in my office that day, Dick leaned forward in his chair and in his inimitable way bluntly asked, "Guy, have you ever thought of unloading the Globe?"

Even though I had been contacted by two potential buyers already, I respected his counsel and always was interested in what he had in mind. So, I rather indifferently asked, "Who could possibly get the money to buy a printing plant in this economy?"

There was no hesitation. "I know two," he said.

"Who might they be?"

I was totally unprepared for his response. "You're looking at one." I nearly fell off my chair! Then he said, "And if we can't cut a deal, I know someone else who can."

A Miraculous Provision
The message was unmistakable. After seventeen years of ownership, without even one serious offer to buy, *suddenly five positive offers are made within a one-month period*, in spite of a distressed economy, and without even a hint to anyone that I might be interested in selling. Only the Lord knew about my interest, no one else! Not even Esther.

Equally as important to me, is that by the time we closed the sale, the Lord helped us restore all but a few clients, get current with every creditor, and rebuild a stable threshold from which my friend, as the new owner with special expertise in sales, now could move the business forward. There could be no doubt about it. The Lord quietly orchestrated the entire transaction.

Something More
One of the attorneys at closing said it best. He remarked that during his career he had put together a lot of business deals. But, never had he done one as large and as complex as ours, absolutely without hassle and

within such a short time. There was clearly something more behind this transaction, he commented, beyond the friendship of seller and buyer. And, indeed, there was!

Quietly, imperceptibly —without voice, vision, dream or demonstration— the Lord illustrated again in our personal lives that He cares. There are no surprises to Him. He orchestrates the high points of our prosperity and moves to extract some good from downside illnesses, twisted circumstances, or betrayed relationships. Even when His silence is deafening and the clamor of circumstances confusing, it's a mistake to forget our Lord is, nevertheless, at work. He knows how to take care of His business...and ours!

CHAPTER **20**

An Unseen Energy-Source For Leadership

If you are in leadership of any kind, there is solid reason for you to be encouraged, in spite of the pressures that occasionally seem to squeeze the life out of you. Hardly anyone in leadership, from Sunday School Teacher to denominational official, floor supervisor to corporate CEO, hasn't felt at times as though he has been thrown into a lions' den like Daniel or a Hell-hot fiery furnace like the three Hebrew children.

Perhaps your enemies are strong and your friends silent. And a sense of betrayal hangs over your broken spirit like a suffocating blanket. Not a few veterans from Bunyan's "slough of despond" have said the disillusionment, disorientation and darkness of such times is incredible. And one usually suffers alone.

But the good news is you are *not* alone!

I've served the church for more than forty years, at virtually every organizational level. More than once, as we worked at conflict resolution, I witnessed events that forced the conclusion that God was around - unseen, but present and supportive!

Perhaps to break through the rigid focus and emotional confusion of such times, -at least in my experience- He occasionally chose a very dramatic way to grab my attention and provide the "booster shot" I needed. And I must tell you: as unusual as the events were, they certainly are not theory. They are authentic history. They happened to me!

An Indian Woman's Dream
I had the pleasure of one of those "booster shots" during a rather stressful period. It occurred while sitting at dinner one Sunday in the home of Pastor Anthony Spero of Glen Burnie, Md.

Joyti Komanapalli and his wife, Asha, a newcomer from India, shared a startling dream with us. About a week before my arrival, Asha awakened one morning and her first words to her husband before getting out of bed were, "Who is BonGiovanni?"

Joyti was stunned by the question and asked, "Where did you hear that name?"

Asha explained she heard the name in a dream.

It seems that in the dream she and her husband were facing a need. As they inquired for help, somebody told them in the dream, "Brother BonGiovanni will help you." At that point Asha awakened. Again she asked her husband, "Who is BonGiovanni?"

"You will meet him in a few days," Joyti assured her. "He is coming to the church for meetings."

Frankly, I don't know who was more mystified by the dream, Esther and I or the Komanapallies! Joyti said he hadn't mentioned my name to Asha. And certainly we had not met before. None of us knew the significance of the dream. But its clearly delivered the reassuring message that God hadn't forgotten my name!

There could be but one response to the dream. "I really don't know what it all means, or if there is any way I can be of help to you," I said to this fine couple. "But, I want to assure you, should you ever experience need, we will certainly do whatever we can to be of help."

Of course, the future will unfold the purpose of the Lord in this obviously supernatural happening. But for the present, whatever other significance Asha's dream might have, one thing is indisputable: it was a powerful reminder that God knows where I am and that He is in control. And that helps!

A Word From The Lord

As I mentioned, over the years I've served at virtually every level of church administration - committees, camp boards, ministerial alliances, denominational district and national offices, etc. For the most part it's been exciting and fulfilling. (I served the Farrell Christian Assembly -now, First Assembly of God- for seventeen years; and I don't even need one hand to count the altercations over that long tenure!) But, as a leader, there have been a few occasions when I needed something special. And the Lord was faithful in providing it.

I can tell you of one occasion, during which I was presiding at a conference, and the climate became unusually stressful. I desperately needed the Lord's Grace and help. Fortunately, help did come. But it came in a manner as unusual as the occasion was stressful.

There could be no question that this was a supernatural happening. It was the Lord's way of reassuring me that His hand was on my life. It was as though God was saying, "I know what's happening and I'll take care of it."

The Lord's instrument in that occasion was a young, but unusually mature, minister serving a significant church in a distant city. In fact, I had only occasional interaction with him. He tried to reach me by telephone, but couldn't get through. Desperate to reach me in some way, the Brother telephoned my wife.

"Sister BonGiovanni," he said, "I need to get a message to Brother Guy. I believe God has given me a message for him. I don't know what's going on, but I feel very strongly that he needs it right now. Perhaps you can get the message to him."

Esther jotted the message down as he dictated it, and immediately reached me. I wrote it down. It was a clear word of encouragement; a reassurance that the Lord knew what was happening and that He would take care of me during this volatile time.

You have no idea how refreshing and reassuring that message was! More than once during the hours that followed, because of the pressure, I yielded the gavel to a colleague and excused myself from the conference table. That was something I rarely did in my years of administration. In the privacy of the men's room, I read and re-

read that message. It gave me a fresh injection of invigorating reassurance and strength to complete my work.

The nature and mannerism of the young minister, who was God's instrument that day, are such one never would expect this kind of thing from him. That, of itself, was enough to reassure me that God knew where I was, what I was going through, and that He was in control, in spite of what was happening. The message was helpful —very, very helpful!

It's difficult to fix a value on this kind of help, that is obviously supernatural, when a leader is held captive in the heat of controversy. Fortunately, our Lord knows we need it, and when necessary, provides it; particularly, when a controversy stretches out over a long time. Such reminders of His care are powerful "booster shots!"

An Unnerving Alert

On another occasion, I was trying to solve some administrative problems with several of my colleagues. During that time I was given one of the most pointed "alerts" of my ministry. Every effort I put forth to initiate dialogue on the issues only strengthened intransigence and intensified hostility. (Christians do get angry, at times, you know! That doesn't make it right. But the reality is, it happens.)

It was a highly pressured time. And it quickly became apparent that nothing short of unqualified capitulation -without dialogue- might defuse hostility. Unfortunately, I couldn't accommodate the situation, even if I wanted to for the sake of peace.

As sincere as my colleagues might have felt themselves to be, their position was perceived to be both Biblically untenable and organizationally unconstitutional. With a few exceptions, I prefer to believe it to be a sincere misconception. But God only knows.

It was during those days that a colleague from a distant city visited one of my Brothers-in-law. He told my Brother-in-law he had a real concern for my well-being and wanted to talk with me. He had received some unusual insight from the Lord, he said, and felt obligated to share it with me. My Brother-in-law telephoned immediately.

To say the least, what this minister told me was unnerving. While in prayer, a vision came to him that spoke to my situation with a clarity and detail that it's not expedient for me to express, although the man of God candidly shared it with me. (Writing about it even now, sends a shudder through me!)

This man had no way of knowing the matters we were trying to resolve at that time. Yet, the things he said had an uncanny accuracy. It was remarkable! The man, who is well known for the accuracy of such revelations, came to my Brother-in-law's home with that word from the Lord *before* either of us had a chance to talk with him. It's said, "truth is often stranger than fiction." This surely seemed to fit that description! At the time I could only wonder what all this meant.

Like Mary, the Mother of Jesus, who also received an unusual word from the Lord, I "hid these things in (my) heart," reassured that this revelation of the Lord also carried with it the comforting promise of His care. Unfortunately, it wouldn't be long until the revelation received from this man of God, would unfold in such a manner that its credibility would be certified as a word from the Lord for me.

"A Voice In The Night"

Perhaps the most dramatic illustration I can give of our Lord's sensitivity to stresses of leadership, involved a Brother who drummed-up spurious allegations against me, and set in motion forces destined to cause a lot of pain.

Later he retracted the allegations; and confessed he wrote them in reactionary anger when I stepped down from what I concluded had become a dysfunctional Committee. But "the die was cast" and the Brother couldn't stop what he started.

As the controversy progressed, the Brother reported he couldn't sleep. He told me that every night he would lay awake praying, "Lord, do something about Brother BonGiovanni. Do something about Brother BonGiovanni."

One night he had a shocking response to his prayer. It jerked him into a sitting position on his bed, it was so forceful. "*You* do something about Brother Bon-Giovanni !" is what he heard.

"I can't say that it was a voice," the Brother said to me. "But I can't say that it wasn't." Whatever it was, he knew he had heard from God, and that he had to do something to help resolve the problem he started.

The next day, he shared his experience with a colleague, and his intention to visit with me to make things right. But, he was strongly dissuaded, even though he had retracted his allegations.

It was an intimidating confrontation for the man. For whatever reason -economic security, peer approval, or whatever- he took it no further. But the Lord wasn't through with him.

"The Finger of God"

Not many weeks later at his office, as he walked past a colleague standing in the foyer chatting with a Pastor from the area, the Pastor suddenly turned toward him, stretched out his arm and pointed his finger at him. Raising his voice to an authoritative level he said, "Brother, you need to get together with Brother BonGiovanni! You have some things to talk over." That was all.

The man was stunned! He said It was like the finger of God pointing right at him. First a voice; now the finger of God! Indeed! Because it's a serious thing to taint a person's reputation (Proverbs 22:1).

Later he told me, right then and there, he made up his mind. Whether or not his associates approved, he would talk with me because he must "answer to a Higher Power." And he did, without telling the men he worked with, until months later.

As we lunched privately, and secretly, the Brother made it right with me. "My anger clouded my judgment," he confessed. "I didn't think it would go this far."

Although he never did muster courage enough to take a stand alone, *publicly*, it became known that in the time he had, before his unexpected and sudden death at an early age, he did what he could to bring his associates to conclude redemptively, the controversy he had initiated.

It's difficult not to respect this man's response to the Lord's supernatural "visitations" and the efforts he put forth to correct his error. His response to the Lord's direction and remedial efforts, indeed, must command the respect of anyone who is committed to forgiveness and reconciliation.

"Bureaucracy" Is Not a Bad Word
I would like to make it clear, notwithstanding the pain at times experienced in working with the "establishment," that "bureaucracy" is not a bad word. Whether beauracracy is good or bad ultimately depends upon those within it; particularly, its leadership. One must also consider that sometimes even good men become entrapped by "group think" and lend their influence to attitudes and actions they otherwise would oppose.

In this respect, the religious world is no different than the secular world. The abuse of bureaucracy is, in fact, so pervasive in society, that no profession or vocation completely escapes its tyranny. Without excusing leadership for its deficiencies, the bottom line requires of us understanding, forgiveness and grace. All of us are still "under construction." We haven't yet arrived! But, hopefully, we are "In *Pursuit of Excellence.*"

We must remember the Lord "keeps the books." He is in control. In His own way and time, issues that concern us will be settled properly, if not in our generation, then at the Judgment Seat of Christ (I Corinthians 3:12-15; 4:1-5). In the meantime, if you will walk sincerely before the Lord, you will find our Lord will send along His messengers of encouragement, with just enough of the supernatural to assure you, indisputably, that He is, indeed, with you.

CHAPTER **21**

What To Do When The Lights Go Out

Few people are spared passages through unexpected darkness. A prognosis of cancer, Aids, or other terminal or disabling disease; the collapse of one's financial stability; the fracturing of relationships held dear; or other events of different, but equally devastating description, can quickly turn the lights out.

It plunges one into darkness that often numbs the mind, deafens the ear, and isolates the victim. But, it sets the stage for a supernatural happening!

None of this is a surprise to our Lord. All of it is part of a world less than what He intended for us. He was candid in saying, "In the world ye shall have tribulation." But He went on to assert, "I have overcome the world" (John 16:33).

Now, that's good news! But the crucial thing is to learn how to identify with that wonderful victory. You might begin with some of these ideas.

1. Keep cool! The worst thing one can do when the lights go out, is panic. Frantically thrashing about for some relief or rationale is as certain to increase your chances of going under as the drowning person who fights against his intended rescuer. A quiet spirit is best. "In quietness and in confidence shall be your strength," has proven to be good counsel (Isa.30:15). Your survival equipment works best in a calm environment. Criticism, blame, bitterness and anger only short-circuit the light even more, and sometimes irreparably fuse the wires causing terminal darkness.

2. Get your bearings! Try to access where you *really* are. That could be quite different from where you *think* you are. So, it's helpful to talk with a trusted friend or two who can help evaluate the darkness, its cause and cure; and also monitor your response to it. A second opinion is valuable. It's now recommended before any major medical decision. Advice from a financial planner might help you avoid economic bankruptcy. You need to determine carefully whether there is anything you can be do to walk safely out of the darkness or whether you really need a miracle to get the lights turned on again in your life.

3. Do what you know to do! When darkness falls, the temptation is to quickly "turn it over to the Lord." Of course one must quickly bring his problem to the Lord, and an attitude of dependence upon the Lord is crucial, elementary and indispensable. Yet, one can "turn it over to the Lord" *prematurely.* To do so either in despair or in avoidance of what one knows he can do to change things if he has the courage to do it, but refuses to do so, only hinders the light.

If you've lost your job, don't just sit there expecting God to rehire you! Get your resumes out! You need to do what you know to do. Anything less is a cop-out of your responsibility. If the diagnosis is terminal, "call for the elders of the church"(James 5:14). Our God is still in the business of reversing even the darkest prognosis of the physician! If a relationship is shattered, " go and tell" your brother "between thee and him alone"(Matt.18:15).

God will do what He *needs* to do. You must do what you *know* to do. Darkness often increases in direct ratio to one's avoidance of responsibility. You can prevent that from happening by doing what you know you should do. The medicine is good for you. Take it!

4. Hold on tight! When darkness falls, it's what's on the inside that counts. Perhaps you can't see the tip of your nose, but your inner "gyroscope" keeps your equilibrium. Even if you can't see the landing lights, it prevents dipping your wings dangerously either to the left or right. It levels you off, for a straight flight through pitch darkness to a safe landing.

The Apostle Paul put it this way: "I know whom I have believed, and am persuaded that he is able to keep that which I have committed unto him against that day"(2 Tim. 1:12). He was aware life's mysteries require that believers exercise not only faith that *receives*, but also faith that *commits*.

His own commitment was solidly based on what the Apostle *knew* about our Lord. He *knew* Him to be good; that He is love; that He is faithful; that He cares. *That* kind of a God was in control! When beaten, stoned, imprisoned or demeaned, Paul just held on tight! Whom He knew God to be, gave him the stability he needed.

Paul's relationship to the Lord was something like that of the little boy walking hand-in-hand with his Daddy in the basement of their home when suddenly a fuse blew and they were plunged into darkness. "Are you frightened son?" asked the concerned Father.

"No, Daddy!" answered the young lad with obvious confidence. "I can't see you. But it's okay as long as I hold on tight."

"Life is not always fair," Robert Schuller reminds us. "But God is good!" We just have to hold on tight. Jacob wouldn't let go until the angel of the Lord blest him (Gen. 32:26). Adonijah "caught hold of the horns of the altar" in the Old Testament temple, and refused to let go until he was assured his life would be spared (1 Kings 1:50). Commitment that holds on like this invites supernatural intervention.

5. Get in the best "position!" Businessmen talk a lot about "*positioning.*" That's just a matter of being in the best possible position to market one's product. One could say the little boy was "positoned" well to cope with the sudden darkness, because of his *relationship* to his Daddy - he was close to Him!

If you are familiar with the Bible, you probably realize God's blessings come to people, either because of His mercy, or because of His Covenant. Humanity, in general, is blest through His mercy. But people who enter into Covenant with God, receive His blessings because they are especially *related* as members of God's Family.

The desperate mother, wanting healing for her daughter, that Matthew tells us about, recognized this *relational* difference (Matthew 15:21-28). When our Lord tested her sincerity and faith by saying, "It is not right to take the children's bread, and to cast it to dogs," our Lord was addressing the matter of "positioning."

The woman realized she was not in the best position to deserve healing because she had no Covenant -or family- relationship with God. She was an outsider! At the same time, she knew God to be merciful. She threw herself upon His mercy saying, "Truth, Lord; yet the dogs eat of the crumbs which fall from their master's table."

The point is, when the lights go out, it's smart to be in the best position possible for God's supernatural intervention. And if you aren't sure you are a member of the Family of God, make sure right now. There can be no doubt about it, your prospects for a miracle are best as a member of the Family of God. And there's no good reason not to become a member of the family of God.

How to become a member of the family of God, is clearly stated by the Apostle John. "But as many as receive him (Jesus Christ), to them gave he power (authority - the right) to become the children of God" (John 1:12). Why hope, as an outsider, for a "crumb" of

God's mercy, when, as a child of God, you can relax in the provision of His Covenant? Like the little boy, people who receive Christ, can be confident it's going to be all right, no matter how dark it gets because they are part of the family of God! Negative attitudes and actions can also short circuit the power of God; so, get rid of them by asking the Lord's forgiveness and help.

6. Rest in the Lord! The Apostle put it this way, "And having done all, to stand"(Eph. 6:13). The lights were out. He had done all he knew to do. There really wasn't anything more he could do. Now it was God's turn! It was up to the God he knew to be faithful. Like Moses, Paul would now "stand still and see the salvation of the Lord"(Ex.14:13). He was confident that although his God might not always work by His omnipotent power to remove the darkness, He certainly does always work by His wisdom. Paul rested in that great fact. So, can we.

Two things more must be said about those scary times when the lights go out: *1.) Darkness isn't always bad, and it isn't all bad.* Whether to grow truffles that titillate the palate of the gourmet connoisseur, or to provide an environment in which stunning images of dazzling color can emerge from a photographer's film, sometimes darkness does serve a good purpose. It can even have a calming affect on an Apostle's spirit that races with the excitement of special revelations (2 Cor. 12:7). "Treasures of darkness" can be mined from the worst of life's experiences (Rom. 8:28). One of your special challenges will be to find them.

2.) *Remember!* *The sun will shine again.* That's not easy to keep in focus when one's body stings with pain or the sheriff is at the door. But darkness is the prelude to the dawn! And it always does come, eventually. It will for you, too.

"Instruments Of God"
Time and *means* are the instruments of God for the help of man. Neither pharmaceuticals nor exercises are adversaries of miraculous deliverance (1 Tim. 4:5; 5:23). Deliverance can be *immediate* (Matt. 8:3; Acts 3:7); *progressive* (Mark 16:18; Luke 17:14); or *deferred* to the new body one shall receive in the resurrection (1 John 3:2; 1 Cor. 15:52, 53). It is no less an act of the atoning grace of God should He choose to deliver one in Heaven by ushering him through the portals of his eternal Home, as it is should He choose to deliver from terminal illness or other tragedy by a miracle on earth.

Things can't get much darker for you than they did for Habakkuk. And Job, that venerable old man of adversity, was like a pit bull in his commitment. "Though (God) slay me," he said, "yet will I trust in him" (Job 13:15). These historical icons of suffering kept believing the sun would shine again.

The day brightened for Habakkuk as he affirmed, "The Lord God is my strength, and he will make my feet like hinds' feet, and he will make me to walk upon mine high places" (Hab. 3:19). Job lost everything he had. But history records he got it all back, and then some! "The LORD gave Job twice as much as he had before" (Job 42:10).

Within the last year, Al Gerba, a beloved member of our church was hospitalized for cancer of the esophagus. He underwent the usual chemo therapy and eventually surgery. The prognosis was not encouraging. Al was hospitalized and bedfast for months. But Pastor Larry Haynes led the congregation in "praying without ceasing" for him.

At one point, Al went into something like a coma, and for days gave no sign of awareness. He was on life support systems. But the congregation didn't give up!

Actually, we really don't have a right to give up. No one has a right to give up on trusting God for someone's healing or deliverance until there is no longer any reason to believe for it. Only one of two things signals that point. They are healing or death. Until then, we are to pray for healing(James 5:14).

Eventually, Al regained consciousness. The process of healing began. In a remarkable way, his health is being restored progressively; yet, no less miraculously. And he is home again! Even his walking ability which had been impaired by muscles atrophied from being bedridden for so many months, is being restored with therapy.

That glorious resurrection power of Christ again bore witness to the Word which asserts, "if the Spirit of him that raised up Jesus from the dead dwell in you, he that raised up Christ from the dead shall also quicken (make alive) your mortal bodies by his Spirit that dwelt in you" (Romans 8:11).

When the lights go out, what we need more desperately than a fixing of the problem, are the attitude and the outlook described by the Apostle Paul to the Roman Christians. It's a triumphant perspective; and it can provide the upbeat we need until the lights go on again:

(35) "What shall separate us from the love of Christ? Shall tribulation, or distress, or persecution, or famine, or nakedness, or peril, or sword?.... (37) Nay, in all these things we are more than conquerors through him that loved us. (38) For I am persuaded that neither death, nor life, nor angels, nor

principalities, nor powers, nor things present, nor things to come, (39)Nor height, nor depth, nor any other [creation], shall be able to separate us from the love of God, which is in Christ Jesus, our Lord" (Romans 8:35-39).

In My Lifetime: An Odyssey of Supernatural Happenings

*" Therefore I say unto you,
Take no thought for your life,
what ye shall eat,
or what ye shall drink;
nor yet for your body,
what ye shall put on.
Is not the life more than meat,
and the body than raiment?
Behold the fowls of the air:
for they sow not,
neither do they reap,
nor gather into barns;
yet your heavenly Father feedeth them.
Are ye not much better than they?.
...But seek ye first the kingdom of God,
and his righteousness;
and all these things shall be added unto you."*
Matthew 6:25,26,33

EPILOGUE I

Exclusive...
To The Thinking Person

God does good things for people just because He is good. He cares for us like a good Father should, and sees to it that what we need —and often, what we *want*— is provided for us. That's the message of Jesus recorded by Matthew when he wrote "All these things shall be added unto you," of the person who will "seek first the kingdom of God, and his righteousness..." (Matthew 6:33). This was said by our Lord in reference to some very material concerns like "What shall we eat? or, What shall we drink? or, Wherewithal shall we be clothed?" (v.31).

Our Lord is deeply concerned that we shall have sufficient to eat, drink and clothe ourselves. As a matter of fact, any anxiety over these matters should be negligible to His followers because they are *family*. In contrast, "after these things do the Gentiles seek" (v.32), He explained, inferring that

Gentiles (or, people unrelated to Him, except through creation), need to be concerned about their personal well-being. Apart from the general care of God for His creation because of His mercy, there is no *relational* basis for *Gentiles* to expect any special attention.

A Matter of Relationship

It's much different for a Christian. Because of our Covenant (Family) relationship with Him, Christians can be confident our Heavenly Father will take especially good care of us. As yet, *Gentiles* haven't come into a family relationship with God. So, they need to fend for themselves. In contrast, our Heavenly Father takes good care of us. We are family by choice and by Covenant!

Sometimes, the Lord does good things just to get our attention. Jesus referred to the works of God as "signs." Among His last words to the disciples while on earth, our Lord said, "And these signs shall follow them that believe." Then, He listed several attention getters, ranging from a supernatural ability to speak in languages one has never learned to laying hands upon sick people and watching them recover (Mark 16:17-18).

Why "Unusual" Things Happen

The purpose of these and other supernatural expressions of the Lord, including many that you have read about in this book, is not simply to help the people involved - although that's important to God, too- but more importantly, to provide evidence that the message Christians proclaim is really of God, and hopefully to influence them in becoming members of the family of God.

It was incredible to the Apostle Paul that his Jewish friends should miss this basic rationale for supernatural happenings. He expressed it in his letter to the Romans when he wrote, more from a sense of embarrassment than as a serious question, "(Don't you know) God's kindness is meant to lead you to a change of heart?" (N.E.B.,v.4).

Don't Disengage Your Brain!
Unfortunately some folks have the idea that for one to be a Christian he must be ugly, poor and stupid. Even though there are some mysteries we can't understand, at no point in the process of faith, does our Lord expect a person to disengage his brain! Nor take vows of poverty or sacrifice beauty.

It's significant that Jesus did not censor Thomas when he refused to believe until he had solid evidence of His resurrection.

Rather than being offended by Thomas' demand for evidence, eight days later, Jesus graciously accommodated his questioning mind and provided empirical evidence that He, indeed, was real (John

20:24-28). It was the historical church, not Jesus, that tagged Thomas with the infamous label, "*Doubting*" Thomas.

No Premium On Stupidity

Jesus respected Thomas' intellectual search —as He does all *sincere* skepticism— and moved to satisfy it. That "inquiring minds want to know," is not a contemporary nuance. Our Lord puts no premium on stupidity. So, at times, He both captures our attention and validates His Message with the things He does for us *supernaturally* —things that "confirm" the reality of the Christian Faith (Mark 16:20). And although we might not understand "all mysteries," the persuasive power of the supernatural can solidly anchor one's faith in the reality of Jesus (1 Cor. 2:4,5).

When I hear about, or experience for myself, God's extraordinary works, if I am at all a thinking person, I can't help but ask, "What's it all about?" And in that moment, God's "signs," have fulfilled their purpose! Just like Moses, who was attracted by a bush that "burned with fire, and the bush was not consumed." He turned aside to "see this great sight" (Exodus 3:2,3).

God Gets Our Attention

Now, God has my attention; and if I will let Him, He will lead me into a genuine relationship with Himself. Jesus affirmed that, "If any man will to do his (God's) will, he shall know of the doctrine, whether it be of God" (John 7:17). In other words, the Lord will lead one into a genuine relationship with Himself, if one is honest about it.

The "signs" of supernatural happenings force me to conclude there must be more to life than my own humanity. If I'm to be intellectually honest, I need to explore it. Integrity demands it!

Logically, this will lead me to the Bible, since this is a religious concern. Now one can argue all day about whether or not the Bible is really God's Letter to humanity. But the fact remains, irrefutable proof of the fact exists even though there are some things we can't fully explain. But then, we aren't God, are we? So, we move forward on the premise that the Bible is God's Word, confident that the witness of brilliant men both in theology and science support the premise.

Real New Birth Or Phony Jesus

If we are to pursue faith sensibly, and unless we are ready to make the preposterous judgment that Jesus was a phony, we must deal with the fact that *He* said, "Except a man be born again, he cannot see the kingdom of God" (John 3:3). There can be no question about it. W*hatever* this New Birth is, we *must* have it or we can't have a right relationship with God and the assurance of eternal life. The consequences of either neglecting or rejecting it are too serious to be taken lightly.

Actually Jesus' comment was a "flashback" to what happened shortly after God created the first person, Adam. From Sunday School, most people remember when God created man, He breathed into him the breath of life (singular), because that's the way it's translated in the King James Translation. The word actually is *lives* (plural), a *complete* or *whole* person (Genesis 2:7). With great care, God warned that something would die inside Adam should he *choose* to violate the regulations God established for Adam and Eve's wellbeing.

Unfortunately, Adam failed the Lord and something, indeed, did die inside him. And although humanity has achieved remarkable pinnacles of goodness through the centuries, without benefit of an inner life that connects him to his Creator, the depth of his savagery at the same time has eclipsed the good that's been done and bears witness to his self-imposed alienation from God.

Missing "Parts"
It happens because something crucial is missing! The Apostle Paul recognized the fact and wrote of it to the Corinthians: "The natural man receiveth not the things of the Spirit of God: for they are foolishness unto

him: *neither can he know them,* because they are spiritually discerned" (1 Cor. 2:14).

Don't miss the segment I've italicized! It holds a key to understanding what's happening in society today. People lack the equipment for really *understanding* spiritual things, let alone for living like they should! And it must be restored if one is to be rightly related to God and live better.

That's why Jesus said *everybody* must be Born Again. He wants to replace what Adam lost! When God created man, He GEnerated him with spiritual life; when Adam disobeyed God, his spiritual life was DEgenerated; now through commitment to Jesus Christ, man can be -really *must* be- REgenerated; so that, his spirit once again can spring into full life, equipping him to both understand and receive what God has for him.

An Intelligent Decision

That's a personal experience you must have if you expect to be rightly related to God -become a member, not of a church, but of the family of God- and live life at its best. But it doesn't just happen. You must allow it to happen by an intelligent, deliberate decision with respect to Jesus Christ.

What brings the New Birth to you is how you respond to what Jesus has done for you; particularly, when He died on the cross. As ugly as crucifixion was, I don't know of anything for which we must be more grateful. And here's why.

I really don't have to tell you we "all have sinned, and come short of the glory of God," unless your sense of honesty has been totally distorted (Romans 3:23). Our sin has been an impregnable barrier to a good relationship with God. There was absolutely no way we could get through it, except for what Jesus did on the cross! Paul was very direct about it: "Christ died for us" (Romans 5:8). Because He died in our place, for our sins, the barrier between us and our Creator has been removed. As a result, we can now come directly to Him to get our spiritual life restored.

If you understand this, I'm sure you will agree two things follow logically. If we *really* recognize Christ died *in our place:*
1) we will sincerely regret our personal sins that made it necessary for Him to die and ask Him to forgive us for them; and
2) we will accept what He did in such an intimate way that we will acknowledge He died on that cross for us *personally*. This is basic and sensible.

Right now, if you can bring yourself, with the help of God, to come to a place of repentance and faith, *at this very moment,* according to the beloved Apostle John, you will be Born Again! What was lost in the Garden through the disobedience of Adam is now restored inside you through the Grace of God in Christ. "But as many as received him, to them gave he power (i.e. -authority, the right) to become the sons of God; even to them that believe on his name: Which were born...of God" (John 1:12,13).

A Sure Thing
The moment you invite Christ to be your personal Saviour, the Bible assures us New Birth happens in you. It might be a very dramatic time for you, or a quiet experience. But it happens! The blockage between yourself and God is removed and you become a new person in Christ Jesus.

He Took Our Place And Paid Our Debt
Because of sin, you —and all of us, for that matter— really should have been separated from God, eternally. But Jesus took our place and we have been spared! "The wages of sin is death, but the gift of God is eternal life through Jesus Christ, our Lord" (Romans 6:23). That's what Christians mean when they talk about being "saved."

We've been saved from the certain death of being separated forever from our Lord. It's a marvelous provision of undeserved Grace for which we must be grateful.

♦

If the supernatural works of God have pointed you in the direction of God's Grace, the signs have fulfilled one of their purposes. You are blessed to understand God loves you dearly. And if you personally recognize Jesus took your place on the Cross, and invite Him into your life, you will now become a member of the family of God!

Perhaps this prayer will help you:
If you are thinking carefully about your personal relationship to the Lord as you read through this, you might find it helpful right now to quietly express yourself to God like this:

"Dear God, the stories I've been reading in this book have helped me think about my personal relationship with You.

"I know I'm no different than anyone else. I understand my sins are a barrier that's been blocking your best blessings from coming to me, and have hindered us from enjoying the friendship that should exist between us. Please forgive me for ignoring you until now; and for the walls between us.

"I also understand now that Jesus took my place on the cross, for my sins. I deeply appreciate what He did for me and I sincerely invite Him into my life.

"Dear God, I want you to hear it from my lips -as well as from my heart- that on this day, I do accept Jesus as my personal Saviour.

"Thank you for making me a new person on the inside. With Your help, and as best I can, I will live in a way that will please you. Amen."

♦

Allow me to make one more suggestion. Now that you have done the right thing, and invited Jesus to be your personal Saviour, it's extremely important that you regularly read your Bible, talk to the Lord, and interact with others who truly love the Lord.

Find people who talk openly and freely about the Lord. (People who are in love aren't embarrassed or ashamed of it!) And if you can't find people you can be comfortable with, write me. I have friends virtually across the nation, and in several foreign countries. I'm sure we can put you in touch with someone. It's crucial that you nurture what the Lord has begun in you. Write: Life Enrichment Ministries, Inc., P.O. Box 543, Hermitage, Pennsylvania, 16159 - 0543 U.S.A.

" *Trust in the LORD,
and do good;
so shalt thou dwell in the land,
and verily thou shalt be fed.
Delight thyself also in the LORD;
and he shall give thee
the desires of thine heart.
Commit thy way unto the LORD;
trust also in him;
and he shall bring it to pass....
The steps of a good man
are ordered by the LORD;
and he delighteth in his way.*"
Psalm 37:3-5, 23

EPILOGUE II

A Bit About Myself

It was a scene I'll never forget. It hadn't happened before, nor ever again. I don't think Mother was even aware that I witnessed it. I stood there in my knickers, cotton shirt and home-repaired shoes in silent awe and confused pain. It was a moment that seemed forever. Even as I reflect on it now, after 57 years, the ache in the pit of my stomach still lingers.

Tears cut long, rambling furrows down Mother's youthful face, as she wept in silence. Her diminutive form bent slightly over the large copper tub resting upon the three-burner table top gas jet stove. As she twisted the maroon and gray blanket with all the strength she had, wringing out the water, the wrenching pain suffered by this tender but tough little lady in her early twenties was dramatically epitomized.

The load she carried was overwhelming. The blight of incurable pernicious anemia drained her youthful energies. Added to this was the burden of privation, imposed by a husband disabled by a back injury during preWelfare days. It was many years later while I was preparing for ministry, Mom fortunately was healed by a supernatural act of God in a service conducted by the Rev. William Branham in Cleveland, Ohio.

Mom came from a long line of business and professional people, having been born the second child of Frank and Gaetana (Orlando) Fera. We understand Grandpa Fera was quite a "world traveler" before he came to America where he labored as a coal miner. Mom had an older sister, Julia, who with her husband, Joseph Pollino, opened a community grocery in Oneida, in the greater Punxatawny, PA. area. They continued in the grocery business when they moved to Jamestown, N.Y., years later. Mom's younger brother, Carmen, was in heavy equipment rigging and later the restaurant business. Mr. John Apa, who was a member of the Farrell Christian Assembly during my pastoral service there, and who had come to America from Cosenza, Calabria, Italy, remembered a statue of Mother's uncle, Luigi Fera, presides over one of the "piazzas" in Cosenza. He was a Senator in the Italian government.

My Dad came to America alone as a young man of 16, in circumstances unique enough to be remembered half a century later by the aged postman whom we encountered by chance in 1967 during a visit to Rocca Valdine, Sicily.

His Father, Grandpa Francesco Bon Giovanni, died in his early forties when gored through the ribs by a bull. He was a private tutor but also raised cattle when the tragedy happened. Dad was only four at the time.

Grandma Petrina (Franzi) BonGiovanni was sister to a medical doctor in Messina, and to an Archbishop of the Catholic church, who actually cared for my dad after Grandpa BonGiovanni's death.

Some years after coming to America, Dad's marriage to Mother was arranged according to the custom of the time. Mother was only fifteen.

The combined strengths of Mom and Dad brought us through the nation's economic depression of '29 and the thirties, his disability, and her illness. A family of seven children, living off the land and hunting for food rather than for fun, near the railroad tracks on the edge of town beyond the last electric pole, and without indoor plumbing, we nevertheless didn't know "we was po' folks" until somebody told us!

We had no radio, telephone or inside bath. We walked the railroad tracks picking up coal for our stoves, planted gardens and hunted for our food. We did some trapping, too, for extra funds and fun. With my brothers, Frank and John, we held a "monopoly" on the news "industry," delivering the daily morning, evening, and Sunday newspapers to the town of Dayton, PA. where the family eventually relocated when I was three months old. Upon her graduation from the Dayton high school in 1942, the family followed my eldest sister, Petrina, and our dad to Niagara Falls, N.Y. where both had found employment.

The sense of God's hand upon my life intensified, and after working in several family business enterprises and a couple years as a cabinet maker, I enrolled at Eastern Bible Institute, an Assemblies of God school at Green Lane, PA., now Valley Forge Christian College. There I majored in ministerial studies and upon graduation in 1952, immediately entered the evangelistic circuit, conducting "Great Things For You" crusades, mainly throughout the Northeast.

In 1955 I met and married Esther Calvelli in the Bronx, N.Y., who as I, was the middle child in a family of seven children. Together we traveled in evangelism until our first child, Linda, was born. We were then called to Farrell, PA., where the skills she carried over as a private secretary in the Manhattan offices of the Texas Company, as well as her teaching ability, and musical vocal, piano, and organ gifts, made an indispensable contribution to the achievements we enjoyed during nearly 17 years of pastoral service there, and later to the General Council, Christian Church of North America which we dearly loved and to which we were deeply commited for forty years. Our daughter, Karen, was born in Farrell.

Both our daughters are married. Linda and her husband, Steve, have given us three wonderful grandchildren: Christopher, Abbey and Casey. Steve is partner with his Dad in Pantalone Paving Company. They live in Canfield, Ohio. Linda and Steve are alumni of Evangel College, Springfield, Missouri and are active in Highway Tabernacle in Youngstown, Ohio.

Karen and her husband, Nick Sbano, have given us two wonderful grandchildren: Stacey and Nicholas. They live in Rockledge, Florida where both are employed as instructors in the Rockledge Christian School. Nick is on the pastoral staff at Rockledge Christian Center. Both are graduates of Valley Forge Christian College.

Every Service An Adventure
While in Farrell, the congregation grew through hard work, congregational participa-

tion and innovative approaches for church development. New records were achieved in Sunday School, youth, missions and adult ministries. A new church facility, also, was constructed.

The testimonials in this book eloquently speak for themselves of the supernatural touch of God upon our gatherings. During a chance meeting at the local mall a couple years ago, one of our church members reflected upon our years together. He put it nicely. "Every service," he said, "was an adventure."

But this should not have been unexpected, given the historic beginnings of the church under the leadership of the Rev. Peter Bonafiglia. "Brother Pete," as he was affectionately known, hadn't had opportunities for higher education as his successors. But he knew the Lord and His Word. He loved people and trusted God to move among them supernaturally.

Esther and I visited him and his dear wife, "Sister Mary," in Florida shortly before his Home Going. When we arrived, he immediately launched into a discussion of First Peter, freely quoting large passages from memory.

It was on that occasion, as my predecessor in the Farrell pulpit, he paid me one of the highest tributes of my career. There was no reason for it. We had been engrossed deeply in discussing the Word of God when suddenly, with a twinkle in his eyes, he remarked, "Brother BonGiovanni, I don't lend money to anyone. But if you asked me for money, I would lend it to you." I was puzzled! I had not asked him for money. We hadn't even been talking about money!

As I later reflected on it, I concluded he must have been trying to express confidence and camaraderie in terms keyed to his values. I was stunned by the sudden change of topic and humbled by the tribute of this conservative man.

His self-taught skills as a scholar and preacher of the Bible, as well as his achievements in ministry -which included establishing and simultaneously serving congregations in Farrell, Greenville and Meadville- in spite of the fact that he worked secularly throughout his long career, highlight his profound love for God and people.

To overlook the remarkable contributions of Brother Pete in the founding days of the Farrell Christian Assembly would be a gross injustice to his dedication, and to demean the Calling of the Lord upon his life. I would not be guilty of that oversight!

Even though the congregation had diminished both in number and morale by the time I was called to serve it, an expectation for supernatural happenings had been so deeply engrained within its root system by Brother Pete, that it continued as a strong base in the church for future manifestions of God's supernatural power.

The Farrell congregation was active in interchurch community concerns; and the State Sunday School Association. During my term as president of the Farrell-Wheatland Ministerial Association, we sponsored, to our knowledge, the only city-wide evangelistic crusade in the history of Farrell.

When I was called to direct the Missions Department of the General Council, Christian Church of North America, by the Grace of God, we left a tithing congregation, in a modern facility, and strong in every department. We completed a feasibility study that advised additional expansion to accommodate growth.

We left a well-trained corps of lay leadership that would successfully carry the congregation through several future pastoral transitions. In fact, during our pastoral years there, 13 young men and women followed the Call of the Lord into ministry and enrolled in resident Bible Schools. To our knowledge, only three are not in full-time ministry today.

During the 12 years I served as Executive Director of Missions, I traveled twice around the world, through some 30 countries and negotiated the formation of an international network for the CCNA by negotiating affiliations with a number of national Movements, embracing the Philippines, Australia, India, Italy, North Europe, Barbados, Venezuela, and Argentina.

Introducing and promoting the Faith Promise based missions convention in local churches increased missions giving by more than 500%. The number of appointed North American missionaries also achieved its highest peak in CCNA history.

In September of 1984, the General Council elected me as its General Overseer. A multi-faceted master plan for development known as "Direction" was well-received by the Council. Morale rose sharply, new credential holders were enlisted, new churches affiliated and planted, credential holders were carefully screened and ordained to the ministry during each convention — on one occasion at least 20 were ordained— and renewed recognition was enjoyed in the National Association of Evangelicals and the Pentecostal Fellowship of North America, associations in which I served as a member of their Boards of Administration. Giving also increased by 104% during our first year and maintained that level through my administration until my resignation from office five years later in 1989.

It has been my privilege to speak at conventions for Manna Full Gospel Mission in Amalapuram, India, the Italian Christian Churches of North Europe, the Assemblies of God in Italy, the Italian Pentecostal Churches of Canada, the Christian Churches of Australia, and the Pentecostal Christian Churches of Argentina, as well as at the leadership convention of the Pentecostal Fellowship of North America in Toronto, Canada. Much of my time has also been given for local and regional conferences in churches of various denominations.

At the time of this writing I am a member of the Board of Directors for Elim Bible Institute of Lima, N.Y. I also served as extension faculty for Trinity Bible Institute in St. Louis, MO. During commencement ceremonies at Valley Forge Christian College in 1982, I was honored with induction into the Delta Epsilon Chi Honor Society of the American Association of Bible Colleges. Membership in the Society is by recommendation of the College faculty and is awarded only to graduating students with at least a 3.75 average or alumni of ten years for scholastic and/ or professional achievement.

My articles have been published by *The Pentecostal Evangel,* weekly voice of the Assemblies of God; the *Gospel Herald,* semimonthly magazine published by the Union Gospel Press; *Vista* Magazine of the Christian Churches of North America; and the publications for leadership of the Assemblies of God, USA, and the Pentecostal Assemblies of Canada, respectively, *Advance* and *Resource* Magazines.

In my early years I founded and published, "Christianity," a magazine of applied truth. For several years I was editor of "Power" magazine, the full color monthly voice of the R.W. Schambach ministries. I currently serve as a member of the Board of Directors for that ministry.

My current ministry is reported in the Life Enrichment Ministries "*Resources*" newsletter. Seminars for local churches are presented on Leadership, Family Life, Couple's Concerns, Charismatic Dynamics and other themes to enrich and equip people for abundant living. Institutes for "Excellence in Ministry" also are conducted for sectional ministerial fellowships. This is the Calling of the Lord for my life; and it has been exciting, challenging and fulfilling.

Most young people agonize through an identity crisis as they emerge into adulthood and discover their primary career. It's sort of a fee paid for the right of passage into adulthood, I suppose. Fortunately, by the Grace of God, I was spared that trauma.

From what my mother told me, it appears I had a sense of Call to the ministry -or at least some affinity for it- from my earliest childhood. This is even more significant to me because we really didn't have a heavy religious focus in my early years, although Mother was deeply devoted.

Not only that -and this might come as a surprise to my colleagues- my life-long battle with shyness made public ministry the most unlikely career of choice for me. Most of the time, it's quite difficult for me to casually interact in public settings. (The ministry persona my colleagues know me to be is purely the product of the Lord's gracious anointing upon my life, nothing more!)

As a teenager, I toyed with the usual career fantasies. At one point, I thought I might want to be a forest ranger, getting right down to the simplicity of Mother Earth, exploring the great Canadian Northwest. But I was also challenged with the more adventurous imaginings of "going where no man has ever gone before," exploring our mysterious galaxy!

When I look back on it now, it's quite amusing. In my elementary school autobiography (everyone had to write one!), I actually wrote I wanted to be the first man on the moon! The possiblilty of that was purely fantasy, at the time! And I did my Junior High School career note book on flying for the U.S. Navy. A host of other interests sparkled in my imagination from time-to-time as I grew into manhood.

The one constant in my development, however, was an everpresent, but nonverbalized, interest in the Lord's service. As a young boy I had a visitation from the Lord I can neither define, nor describe. I just know it happened! It happened while sitting with the family in one of those "marathon" devotional periods when Mom and Dad would read the Bible and lead us in prayer after they had committed their lives to Chirst.

That subliminal interest was nurtured, unconsciously, by my own mother's profound, but quiet, devotion to the Lord; later, through the influence of a fine Methodist minister, the Reverend Henry L. Millison, in whose Daily Vacation Bible School, in Dayton, PA., I memorized the Beatitudes, the Ten Commandments and the Love Chapter, 1 Corinthians 13. My personal commitment to Christ in my mid-teens and a later powerful Baptism in the Holy Spirit, left no doubt in my mind in what I should invest my life.

The multiple influences, circumstances and persons that criss crossed my life to enrich me with the gifts and graces necessary for the Lord's service, and progressively launched me into ministry, are a powerful tribute to the dependability of His Word. It assures us, "The steps of a good man are ordered by the Lord" (Psalm 37:23).

The Lord's favor, indeed, has been upon me, my family and the work to which He called me.

I have no regrets.

I would do it again!

So, the odyssey continues....

"Now unto the King eternal, immortal, invisible, the only wise God, be honor and glory forever and ever. Amen (1Timothy 1:17).

An Introduction to....

Guy BonGiovanni, D. Min.

- Ordained Minister of the Assemblies of God
- Husband of Esther Calvelli & Father of Linda Abraham of Canfield, OH & Karen Sbano of Rockledge, Florida
- President, Life Enrichment Ministries, Inc., presenting seminars and publications for leaders & laity
- Leader of the "Roundtable for Excellence in Ministry" & contributing writer for the Youngstown "Vindicator."
- Author: several books and articles for national religious publications
- Developer: The Pastor's Tool Kit, a CD of Diagnostic & Developmental tools; The Faith Promise, a DVD on giving to missions.
- Former Pastoral Assistant to Rev. Jay Alford, Highway Tabernacle, Youngstown, OH.
- Founder/Pastor of Faith Gospel Tabernacle now merged with Expressway Assembly of God, Buffalo, NY; 4 years in Evangelistic Ministry; 17 years as Pastor of the Farrell Christian Assembly, now Hermitage Assembly of God
- Past Director of Missions & General Overseer for the General Council, (CCNA) Christian Church of North America, now IFCA (International Fellowship of Christian Assemblies).
- Former Member: Boards of Administration of the National Assoc. of Evangelicals and The Pentecostal Fellowship of North America
- Ten years on Boards of Directors for Elim Bible Institute, Lima, NY and R.W.Schambach Ministries; also Consultant for The Institute for Motivational Living, New Castle, PA.
- Inductee, Delta Epsilon Chi Honor Society of the American Associations of Bible Colleges for professional achievement-1982.
- Inductee as an Honorary Member of the Sigma Chi Pi, the Honor Society of the Assemblies of God Commission on Christian Higher Education "In recognition of being a graduate with outstanding academic leadership, approved Christian character, and diligent Christian leadership in an Assemblies of God institution of higher learning." - 1997
- Graduate: Eastern Bible Institute. now University of Valley Forge; Studied, Penn State; Doctor of Ministry degree from Logos Christian College & Graduate Schools, Jacksonville, FL.
- 60 + years in Christian Ministry

LIFE ENRICHMENT MINISTRIES, INC.
EMAIL: GuyBon1830@gmail.com WEBSITE: www.LifeEnrichment.us

www.ingramcontent.com/pod-product-compliance
Lightning Source LLC
Chambersburg PA
CBHW061645040426
42446CB00010B/1582